The Human Energy Control Protocols

What You Need to Know About
The Secret Agendas to
Control Your Energy
& Rule the World

Jennifer Hoffman

An imprint of Feed Your Muse Press, LLC
Enlighteninglife.com

Publisher's Note:

This publication is designed to provide accurate and authoritative information in regard to the subject matter covered. It is sold with the understanding that the author and publisher are not engaged in rendering psychological, financial, legal, or other professional services. If expert assistance or counseling is needed, the services of a competent professional should be sought.

THE HUMAN ENERGY CONTROL PROTOCOLS -- What You Need to Know about the Secret Agendas to Control Your Energy & Rule the World

Copyright © 2016 by Jennifer Hoffman

Printed in the USA and distributed by Feed Your Muse Press, LLC. For more information visit us at www.enlighteninglife.com

Feed Your Muse Press, LLC
A Division of Enlightening Life OmniMedia, Inc.
P.O. Box 7076
Lee's Summit, Missouri 64064 USA

ISBN-13 978-0-9821949-9-7
ISBN-10 0-9821949-9-4

Other Titles by Jennifer Hoffman

Books:

30 Days to Everyday Miracles

The Difference Between a Victor and a Victim is I AM

Be Who You Are -- and Fearlessly Live Your True Purpose

Ascending into Miracles – the Path of Spiritual Mastery

Energy Congruence – Life in Harmony (2016)

The E-Business Primer, a Guide to Business in the Digital Age

CDs:

Cord Cutting and Healing Meditation

Chakra Clearing Meditation

Communicating with your Angels and Spirit Guides

Programs:

GPS Business Academy™ Business Advice, Resources &

Training for Startups, Re-starts, and Expanding Empires

High Vibes Living™ Programs

AIM for AWE - Congruent Energy Alignment™

For additional titles please visit www.enlighteninglife.com

DEDICATION

This book is dedicated to the millions of innocent victims of the

narcissistic, malevolent, and sadistic agendas of

governments and organizations

who believe that it is acceptable, ethical, and proper

to inflict misery, pain, and suffering on their populations

in the name of control, power, and greed.

It is written as a source of information for those

who unknowingly live with the effects of

human mind and energy control today,

to educate them so they can end their unwitting participation,

regain control of their lives, and bring justice to those

who have suffered and died in the name of

secret technologies and global tyranny.

They may be unnamed and invisible but they are not forgotten.

FOREWORD

Dear Reader,

This was not an easy book for me to write as it reminds me of a particularly difficult part of my life which, even with what I have learned and can share with you, still contains many unanswered questions, the biggest of which are:

Why do I have no memory of significant parts of my life?
Why was I the victim of secret mind and energy control programs, and
Why me?

This isn't a topic I normally address and it's a topic that is quite personal for me but I believe that sharing knowledge, information, and experience is one of the most powerful gifts I can give to you. So I am opening a discussion that I hope may help you fill in some of the gaps in your life, as this understanding has helped me with mine.

I was an innocent five year old child when my experience with mind and energy control experiments began. I hadn't done anything to anyone, and I certainly didn't deserve to be victimized by a secret government program whose only purpose was, and still is to find ways to manipulate thoughts, actions, and energy.

Neither did any of the other victims of these programs, but that didn't seem to be a consideration for those who thought that human mind and energy control were legitimate ways to give governments an edge in mass population control and manipulation, a ridiculous endeavor with no social merit and no benevolent purpose. In fact, its premises were considered to be so socially unacceptable that the entire program's existence has been hidden from the public and the experiments and results were kept secret by for decades.

Any knowledge of the mind and energy control programs has been exposed by victims, not by the governments and agencies responsible for their existence.

What do they not want us to know about their activities, which are subsidized with our tax dollars, to the tune of trillions of dollars if you consider that they are conducted in multiple secret facilities, built specifically for these purposes, some of them in deep underground military bases (appropriately called DUMB) and by people who are highly compensated for their work?

After suspecting that something had happened to me and not being able to find any answers, I did my own research. And thanks to the corroborating stories of a few brave mind control experiment survivors and people who are willing to risk their reputations and even their lives to reveal the truth (many people have been assassinated for revealing this information) I found information that helped me start piecing the missing details of my life together. You'll read about what I have learned about human mind and energy control programming, its history, objectives, purpose, and its other assorted ugly details.

I don't like the idea of having things done to my body and mind that were so heinous they were removed from my conscious memory so I could not remember them. I may never know the full extent of what was done to me, although some memories are returning, and there are things I may never know because what I can't remember would have to be corroborated with reports and documents, and those files are locked away in secret facilities that the government hopes no one will ever be able to access.

And those who are guilty of these crimes against humanity will never be prosecuted as they work in the highest levels of the government, scientific, and corporate communities.

There is no penalty for those who commit crimes in the name of 'national security', special interests, deviant scientific, 'anti-terrorism', psychological, or psychiatric 'research', or unethical technology. Any records of these tests have been hidden away in the hope they will never be discovered. But justice has a way of appearing at the most inconvenient times and in the most inconvenient ways, so I hope that this book helps shed some light on this ultra secret aspect of the global human mind and energy control protocols and agendas, as has the stories and testimonials of its MKUltra mind control victims.

Whatever you learn from this book, use it to make empowered, powerful changes in your life. Don't waste your time or your energy on being angry, sad, or regretful. Those emotions are part of the grief process but in the long term, they are just as destructive as the programs and experiments that were designed to control you and your energy. In addition to explaining what these programs are and how they work, I offer suggestions for how to release, de-activate, and disempower this technology so you can regain control of your mind, your energy, and your life.

This is a terrible testimonial as to the true nature of the secret activities of governments and science, as well as a warning to us that we can never take our energy, how we think and what we allow ourselves to believe, for granted. Why human energy, our energy, is so important that so much time, effort, and expense has been expended in an ongoing effort to control it was another question that prompted me to explore this issue and write this book, through the voice of my personal victimhood, as an energy savante, and as a very concerned global citizen.

If we were truly of no value to these people they would have destroyed us long ago, they certainly have the capability to do that many times over. But they haven't and instead, they have spent vast amounts of money and dedicated nearly unlimited resources to ultra secret programs whose purpose is to learn how to control human energy. There must be something very special about it and about us if they're willing to do all of that work just to gain access to our thought processes and actions and how to control and manipulate them. What do you think about that?

If you are one of the many thousands of mind and energy control testing victims, you will find hope, encouragement, power, and support here because whatever was done to you can be overcome and you can get your power back, find your joy, and start living your life in a more balanced and fulfilling way. No matter what was done to you, your energy belongs to you and you can reclaim your energetic sovereignty.

I hope that what you read here is empowering, transformational, and helps you consciously and intentionally regain control of your energy, your power, and your life. And that we, as the collective family of humanity, learn to use our energy for the good of all, for peace on earth, for abundance, prosperity, and joy, and to create a world that blesses us and future generations.

Many blessings,

Jennifer Hoffman
February 2016

TABLE OF CONTENTS

The Human Energy Control Protocols

MY STORY

Every author has a story to tell and this is my story. I have always had the uneasy feeling that something had happened to me during my childhood that I could not remember. It wasn't deliberate memory suppression from the trauma of being para- lyzed by a vaccine at age five and being unable to walk until I was nearly eleven years old, or the many hospital stays that I cannot remember, or the lack of photos of me during that time, or any memory of being with my family.

This was something else, an uneasy feeling that a part of me was gone, I was missing aspects of my being, a feeling of incompleteness that I could never understand or explain.

Being able to remember even a small portion of what has, for many decades, been a dark, unknown space in my memory, along with reading about others' similar experiences, was enough to help me piece together a tale of deception, betrayal, lies, and events that point to a web of collusion and conspiracy so unbelievable that if it hadn't happened to me, I would never think it could be true. Writing this book may put my life in danger, as others have been assassinated for revealing activities that governments and secret organizations don't want publicized. But it's a risk I have to take as what I have learned can help many others.

My story begins in November 1963, when I was five years old. I fell down while running and cut my left knee badly enough to require eight stitches. My parents took me to the hospital emergency room where my wound was stitched. I was given a tetanus shot (DPT) and was sent home. Seven days later I was at school and didn't feel good, so my parents picked me up and brought me home. My mother let me lie down on the couch and watched over me as my conditioned worsened and I developed a high fever.

At one point I told her I told her I needed to go to the bathroom and she told me to get up and go. I replied that I couldn't because I couldn't move. My last memory of that day was lying in the back seat of the car, looking at the stars in the sky through the rear window as my parents drove me to the hospital.

It was also my final clear memory of my life until seven years later.

I was hospitalized with Guillain Barre Syndrome, which is an intentionally non-descriptive name for the total physical paralysis that some people experience after receiving a vaccine. I have very few memories of my life from the time of my initial hospitalization in 1963 until 1970, when I could walk again and didn't require constant hospital visits. In fact, I remember almost nothing about what I did, my family, my friends, where I lived, and even going to school. It is a big blank space, which is strange because I have memories from when I was two years old, and I remember my life in vivid detail beginning at age twelve.

But the period from 1963 to 1970, seven years of my life, is mostly gone, with the exception of a few details.

For many years I thought these memory losses were from the trauma of being crippled, as I moved from being totally paralyzed to being in a wheelchair, to walking with leg braces and crutches. It wasn't easy being stared at or whispered about as people wondered what happened to me. They probably assumed that I was just another one of the thousands of alleged polio victims at the time, and was also an unfortunate victim of this disease. But I have an eidetic memory, everything I see, hear, or read becomes an indelible image in my memory that I can recall at will and describe in very specific detail. Although I remembered some details of my childhood, I realized that there were big gaps in time, especially from age five to age twelve, that I cannot remember at all, or that I remember very little of.

And although my mother took many photos of us as children, there is a gap in their frequency and I am not in many of those photos -- where was I? I noticed this one day, while looking at old family photos my mother had given me a few years ago, that there were no photos of me and of my family between 1964 and 1972. I had noticed it before but thought that my mother didn't want to be reminded of the years I was in a wheelchair and wore leg braces as I was recovering from my paralysis, so she didn't take any pictures of me.

But as I began to piece together the timelines in those old photos, I noticed that many events were also missing, like birthdays, Christmas, vacations, and holidays, and a closed door in my memory began to open. I began to remember more disturbing things that I couldn't make sense of because I couldn't tie them to any part of my life. These started as disjointed memories and feelings, fears, thoughts, and snapshots of people and situations that looked like something out of a 1960s spy film.

Then I started to recall scenes from being in the hospital, lying in a dark room and crying, unable to move because I was paralyzed, while a doctor stood over me and talked to me. I also remember needles being stuck in my feet, and of being left alone in the dark for long periods of time. I remember being cold, wet, and shivering so hard my teeth chattered. I remember being shamed and humiliated, so that I felt like I was being turned inside out. I remember being blamed for things, being yelled at, and having fingers pointed at me as I was told I was bad. It's odd because to this day I can't stand to be cold, I don't like having my feet touched, and I despise being yelled at.

And I have almost no memory of my parents or my siblings during those years. Although I must have gone to school and had friends, I remember nothing about them.

Around the age of twelve I became extremely angry and I hated my parents. I started shoplifting in stores, until I was caught leaving a department store with hundreds of dollars worth of clothing hidden in my coat. My parents had to pick me up at the police station and my father was angry with me for potentially ruining his career by getting arrested. I remember him looking at me with in a sad way and felt that it had less to do with my arrest than it did with other things.

Now I wonder if he knew that my anger was the result of what was being done to me, things he was powerless to stop because if nothing else, his career, and our family's livelihood, depended on his compliance and agreement with anything that was being done to me.

We lived in Europe and often went to visit family in the U.S. for summer vacation. But the summer I was eleven years old my brother and sister went to visit family and I was forced to stay home. I remember very little about the two months I was at home, or was I? Whatever happened in June and July of that year is a complete blank. All I remember is August, when my brother and sister came home and we took our annual month long family vacation in France.

My mother told me we moved several times during the missing years and she always had to admit me to the local military hospital for physical therapy. She also told me that I went to a Shriner's hospital during that time. And yet I remember nothing about going to any hospitals, the doctors, nurses, therapists, and other children I met there, what I did, who I met, who took care of me, and leaving the hospitals. Whatever happened to me while I was there was something I wasn't supposed to remember, and I don't remember any of it at all. Does that seem as strange to you as it does to me?

My father became terminally ill and came to live with me when I was nearly thirty. I remember looking at him one day, as he walked up the stairs to his room, the day after he had moved into my house, and having the thought 'He can't hurt me any more'. That puzzled me because I had no idea where it came from. I didn't remember my father hurting me as a child because I don't remember him being around very much at all. And until he moved in with me, as he was terminally ill and dying, I had not seen or had contact with him in nearly fifteen years. Because of his highly secret government work, he was often gone for long periods of time. I did ask him about his work and my past during the final months of his life but he would never discuss the issue and he died with the answers to my questions locked in his mind.

What did he allow the government to do to me, and why? Whatever I could learn to fill the blanks in my memory would not come from him.

There are also big gaps in my memory during my adult life, and although I know that I was married and had children, I cannot remember much about those decades. I don't drink or take recreational or prescription drugs, so what was happening to me that I cannot remember anything? At different times I can remember feeling like I was standing outside of my body, watching myself do and say things and being powerless to stop myself. Then there are the periods that I just cannot remember at all, more vast gaps in my memories in which I know I was physically present but with no memory of what was going on in my life.

During that period there were times where I could feel myself disconnecting from my body, like I was being peeled out of my energy field. This happened any time I was preparing to make a big life change, when I was approaching a life success, or trying to remember my past. On two different occasions, when I worked with a holographic repatterning practitioner and an energy healer, they both noticed, with a great deal of alarm, that when I approached certain memories I would, as they described it, "leave my body." At these times I felt like I was fainting, my conscious awareness closed down and I could feel myself retreating to some inner space and removing myself from whatever was happening around me.

As I later learned, this is a typical response of mind control programming victim when a forbidden memory is accessed, to shut down conscious mind functionality.

I can also remember this happening during periods of great stress, or if I was trying to do things that that were important to me. In retrospect, it was as though I could function within a certain parameter of behavior but I was surrounded by an invisible boundary that I was either afraid to cross or was not allowed to cross. At the time I didn't understand it, could not find the words to describe what was happening, and there was no one I could ask to find out why this was happening. All I had were constant suspicions that something was very wrong and I had no idea how true it was, although I wasn't ready to remember all of the details yet or to face and fix it.

Although I was overjoyed to be a parent, I had a powerful fear that something would happen to my children or that they would be taken from me. I was fiercely protective of them because I didn't want anything to 'be done to them', which is exactly how I felt, and I was incapable of leaving them in anyone's care when they were babies. So I stayed home with them until they were old enough to speak and to let me know if anything happened to them. I struggled with the fear that I needed to watch them, to be close to them, to protect them from a fate that I couldn't identify or put words to. All I knew was that they needed my protection from some unknown, scary, dark element.

But what was I protecting them from and what did I think would happen to them? I was also afraid that they would be sexually abused, but why? I have a vague feeling that I suffered some sort of sexual trauma but I don't think it happened to me with my parents. If I was sexually abused, who did it, when did it happen, and why?

All of my adult life, I felt detached from my own energy and power. Although I was married and had children, and lived what could be described as an average life on the outside, the inner reality was far different. I was often confused, detached, and felt out of control of my life. Over a period of twenty years I married and divorced several times, only to find myself in oddly similar relationships that were dysfunctional and unhappy -- the names and faces changed but the people were the same. Even my divorces were unusual and I had the uneasy feeling that the court proceedings were interfered with by other sources.

I re-started my life several times, hoping to find happiness only to come to the same point each time and everything fell apart. As I later learned, this inability to achieve continuous stability, success, and happiness is one of the facets of energy control programming due to the interference of technology that controls, manages, and siphons energy. It's true, and you'll read about how that works in a later chapter.

I am not sure how I survived that period but I knew it was because of my children. I loved them above everything else and I did all I could to maintain some semblance of normalcy for their sake. It is what saved my life, my sanity, and kept me motivated enough to press forward, determined to get through the darkest times no matter what it took, and to find the answers I needed to figure out what was going on in my life and the feelings, thoughts, and behavior that I knew were being generated by my mind and body but they were not coming from me.

It felt like I was a puppet and someone else was pulling the strings, or that I was on a tether and could proceed to a certain level of success and happiness in my life, and then I would be pulled back. The pattern repeated itself too many times to be accidental, something else was happening to me, controlling me and my energy, and I had no power to stop it. I no longer had a will, I was responding to a set of invisible commands that were being generated by an unseen source. And then there was the constant nagging fear that something would happen to me and that I would disappear into a dark place where bad things would be done to me and no one would rescue me.

In late 2001, while watching the movie *Hearts in Atlantis,* a vague memory was ignited and I was deeply disturbed by the movie's events, but I was not yet ready to know the truth about my childhood because it didn't go any farther than a strong feeling of discomfort. In the movie, Anthony Hopkins plays an intuitive man who befriends a young, intuitive and sensitive boy. Hopkins' character is hiding from what he calls the 'Low Men', government agents who want to capture him so they can harness his intuitive abilities for their own use. At the end of the movie, in spite of his best efforts, Hopkins is found and taken away by the government men. The movie takes place in the 1960s, when the mind and energy control experiments were at their peak.

Then, a few years ago, I began seeing stories about mind control programs, secret experiments conducted by the Nazis during WWII and extended after the war by the US, Canadian and British governments and secret spy organizations like the CIA and its international counterparts. These projects involved men, women, infants, and children, using them to explore the limits of human tolerance to every kind of physical, mental, sexual, and emotional abuse and torture imaginable, testing the effects of mind altering experimental drugs, in an effort to understand how to control the human mind.

With names like Project MK-Ultra, Monarch, Artichoke, Beta Programming, and others, these projects were deemed to be national priorities and were generously funded. Their activities were so heinous, deviant, and abhorrent that they were conducted in absolute secrecy. The term 'brainwash' was introduced at this time, to describe how belief systems could be systematically altered by the use of emotional, physical, and psychological torture, accompanied by mind altering drugs and post-hypnotic suggestion, to erase the memory of what the experiments' victims had endured.

These secret mind and energy control experiments continued for over four decades until information leaks led to inquiries by the same officials who had previously sanctioned the mind control projects. The sparse details that were shared with the public were a small sample of activities whose techniques were so socially, morally, ethically, and politically unacceptable that the files and records describing them and their results were supposedly destroyed by CIA management in the mid 1970s, to avoid public exposure, incrimination, and criminal consequences.

But knowing the excruciating detail that has permeated all Nazi-based activities in the past eighty years, those documents were not destroyed, they're hidden away in secret vaults because the scientists cannot bear to see the results of their work destroyed, while they also hope no one will find them as they continue to expand on this work today.

Then more recently I read Anne Diamond's book, *My Cold War,* an account of her experiences in the secret mind and energy control experiments in Canada, spearheaded by the infamous Dr. Ewen Cameron, who was known for the use of particularly vicious electroconvulsive shock therapy, trauma based treatment, and the heavy use of psychotropic drugs. Many of his patients were damaged for life and he was never prosecuted for his role in spearheading Canada's collaboration in the CIA's MKUltra program.

She also describes her missing memories, altered timelines, and fears and experiences she could not place, including regular weekend trips to clinics and hospitals in remote areas where she vaguely remembers abuse, and physical and emotional torture and abuse, all conducted on groups of young children.

This was the final piece of the puzzle for me and I knew that I had found the reason I was missing so many pieces of my childhood. And as I continued to read about these programs and the troubling victim and survivor accounts, I noticed that they shared a common thread, especially in the experiments conducted on children. They were all from the same generation, all were intuitive, sensitive, intelligent, and their parents were generally in government or military service.

Although I could not imagine that my parents could have allowed that to be done to me, like many victims in that time, my father worked in government service and we received medical care at military hospitals. In fact, my first hospitalization was at the US Army hospital in Frankfurt, Germany, the center of the CIA's mind and energy control network in Europe.

It was not comforting to uncover this information but it did answer many questions I had about my life and childhood that no one could or would answer, especially the most important question -- what happened to me and why can't I remember it?

Now that I have full awareness of my victimization by the mind control testing establishment, I have a new understanding of the fears of my past and they are no longer controlling my life. If this is something you believe has happened to you, once you know the truth, you are free of the control that once ruined your life and was able to manipulate your energy and run your mind.

Why was I chosen for these experiments? I believe, as I'll describe in the next chapter, that I was chosen because I was an exceptionally intuitive, highly empathic, and very intelligent child. And I have discovered that others with similar childhood experiences share these qualities. I am an 'energy savante' and have always been highly intuitive. My first intuitive insight happened when I was two years old, although I didn't know what that was at that time. I am part of a generation of highly intuitive, empathic, and intelligent children born from the mid 1940s to the early 1970s, and they were preyed upon by governments and secret organizations who wanted to find the means to control their energy. And to some extent, they did.

While the experimentation period may have lasted for five to ten years, there were longer term effects that silently continued to control their energy and their lives and they also have lost memories and unexplainable childhood events involving hospitals, psychologists, psychiatrists, and the same patterns in their relationships, how they can live their lives, and a deep fear of unknown origins that limits their ability to feel normal, to be happy, and to be successful.

In the next chapter I'll explain the history of mind and energy control technologies, how they began, what they were designed to do, and how they have evolved today.

Please pay attention to anything that sheds some light on your experiences or that resonates with you because if you think that this is something that happened to you, it probably did. And if there are parts of your childhood you cannot remember, there is probably a very good reason and you may find the answers and clarity you need here. I hope that you do get clarity because in order to reclaim control of your energy you are going to have to understand what happened to it and to assert your ownership over what has always been yours -- your life force, your energy, and your energetic sovereignty in your life -- if you are to over-come what has been done to you and start living your life on your own terms, with your energy intact.

MKULTRA Plus — FROM MIND TO ENERGY CONTROL

If you're wondering why anyone would want to control human energy or human minds, that's a good question. To understand the reasoning behind these activities you have to go back to the pre WWII Nazi era, which is when modern day mind control experiments began. But even prior to that, controlling how people believe and think has been the focus of those who wish to rule over others with absolute financial, economic, and political control, and to remove any aspect of self awareness, motivation, individuality, or self determination from populations so they become obedient, subservient, and capable of being manipulated, doing what they are told to do, when it is convenient for those in charge, fulfilling the whims and desires of their rulers, devoid of any ability to live their lives in their own way as independent free thinkers.

For centuries various popes, kings, queens, emperors, and dictators demanded absolute fealty and obedience from their subjects, believers, and followers, under the fear of persecution and physical or spiritual death. And for many

17

centuries they were successful. But as people became more educated and more aware of different options, they sought their own paths and were no longer willing to subject their lives to someone else's control.

Throughout time small numbers of people have spoken out against domination and control, with marginal success. As larger numbers of people began to want more out of life than tyranny and domination, they began to revolt and protest against the religious, political, and economic limitations that existed for the sole purpose of ensuring that no one got too comfortable, too independent, too secure, or too rich to no longer want to be told what to do. When it became apparent that it was becoming more difficult to control people through basic fear, financial restriction, and intimidation, the field of mind control experimentation was born, which has since evolved to include energy control.

Early mind control experiments, as defined by the Nazis in WWII, were designed to find out how to control human action by controlling the mind and its thoughts. Initially it was believed that if people could be traumatized enough, starting at an early age, their minds would fracture and compartmentalize the trauma, rendering them incapable of maintaining a stable identity and any kind of self awareness. This would turn them into human robots that could be programmed to commit any kind of act without question, who could be used as assassins and human weapons, or as mindless workers who would be willing to work for long hours, at any kind of task, for low pay, and they would never complain.

And this was proven to be mostly true as it has been woven into the fabric of society today. On a subtle level, schools program children to be obedient and do as they are told. Most education systems are based on the nineteenth century Prussian model, which was designed to create obedient soldiers and loyal employees. A teen's first job is generally in a place where conformity, uniformity, obedience, and subservience are required. Where do most teens in the US get their first job? At fast food restaurants where uniforms suppress individuality, strict rules control behavior, and the mindless tasks they perform remove any opportunity for free thinking and, in fact, they actively discourage it.

Many of the Nazi scientists and researchers who were working in the area of mind control, or MKUltra as the Nazis called it, were brought to the US after WWII, in a secret project called Project Paperclip, and given new identities, jobs, and research facilities, at taxpayer expense, to continue their work, many at a facility in Montauk, New Jersey, others at secret facilities around the US, Canada, and the UK.

While the original Nazi MKUltra plans did show some results, the research and experiments were very limited because they had to be done on an individual basis and all individuals did not respond to the testing in the same way. Some were more easily broken, others would not break and had to be killed. And many died from the brutality of the testing methods.

As technology improved, the testing was moved out of the private laboratory and into the public domain. Broader levels of mind manipulation became possible with the availability of movies and television. Film has been used as a method of mind control for decades. For example, the 1920s and 1930s films describing the evils of marijuana were simply an exercise in manipulating public opinion to destroy the hemp industry, which presented a considerable threat to the oil, paper, steel, fiber, and chemical industries. For decades film and television have been used to influence consumer behavior for everything from laundry detergent to fashion, from political parties to child rearing.

The mind control technology used overt and covert messaging, hidden images, embedded imaging, and subtle psychological tools whose purpose was to train the brain to respond to triggers that suggested behavior, mood, responses, and beliefs and it worked very well, for a while. But as people became more self aware and less subject to manipulation and control, the efforts at manipulation had to be increased until they got so blatant that people simply got tired of watching TV and turned it off.

There is only so much reality TV that is tolerable, we can withstand a limited amount of bad behavior on the part of Hollywood icons, housewives, survivors, Jersey teens, and other assorted tools of the daily diet of mind control manipulation fed to us through television.

Then in the early 1990s the mind control experimentation field was expanded again to include the concept of energy control, with the expansion of research that had been conducted in conjunction with mind control programs, experimenting with the use of different energetic frequencies used in conjunction with energy broadcasting technology to access the human brain, inducing behaviors and affecting physical health.

It has been proven that energy control technology has the ability to override the body's natural and organic processes and control all body functions by hijacking the body's energy frequency. This technology exists and has been the subject of a wide variety of patents for over fifty years, and it has been continuously used on the general population for decades. It is not something that is a work in progress and that will be used some day, it is being used today, and it is being used on you right now, although you are not consciously aware of it.

Mind control experiments have added the energetic component to expand their ability to control, manipulate, and exterminate people. A variety of energy control experiments have shown that technology can be used to implant thoughts to literally 'tell' people what to do by putting words in their head. Others use low level energy to control behavior, physical well being, and mood.

The more sinister energy control experiments are designed to control, eliminate, or manipulate all aspects of the essence of humanity, the human emotions such as motivation, determination, compassion, empathy, kindness, and love, so humans could be trained as assassins and robots, responding to any type of orders without question.

Mind and energy control technologies are designed to control behavior, thinking, and actions, through radio and sound waves, modulated energy frequencies delivered via implanted devices in the body, as well as ground and air based tools and technologies sending out specific types of energetic frequencies with the ultimate goal of active mass population control by remote means.

The ultimate goal of these experiments was to have total control over human populations, so they would automatically respond to the will and instructions of whoever was controlling the energy technology. Humans could be remotely manipulated to fight or surrender, be healthy and strong or die, eat or have no appetite, sleep or suffer from insomnia, spend money or hoard it, depending on the commands given by the energy frequency output levels. Energy technology is designed to reduce human will to a malleable pulp that is capable of being mass controlled by remote means.

There is a type of energy technology which is designed to create 'super humans', according to the Aryan model designed and promoted by the Nazis during WWII, and eliminate every-one else. If you think that's far fetched, don't laugh because the technology that can do this already exists and this is already in progress. In their most powerful forms, they are weapons of mass destruction, capable of annihilating mass populations before they even know they are dead. More powerful than gases or bombs, their results are quick, invisible, deadly, and pinpoint accuracy is not required. A single blast of high intensity microwaves can do the same thing to a human body that it does to a bag of microwave popcorn or a marshmallow.

The experimental techniques used in mind control experiments were first developed by the Nazis and involved sensory deprivation, hypnosis, powerful mind altering and psychotic drugs, torture, physical and sexual abuse, and other methods specifically designed to be so horrific so as to induce such severe trauma that the mind would become a malleable tool, fracturing itself to compartmentalize the trauma and remove the conscious connections to basic emotional functioning. The subjects were men, women, and children of all ages, races, and cultures.

Today MKUltra, Monarch, Montauk, and similar programs are still   being conducted in secret, as is the torture and abuse of thousands of babies, children, and adults, by governments who continue to seek the means to control the minds and energy of their people for their own twisted ends. These have been written about extensively in the past decade although their existence has long been kept a secret from everyone except those involved.

But they have also been expanded to include new methods and technologies to help them overcome the limitations of simple mind control, which didn't offer a broad enough spectrum of use and was too narrow in scope. The need to use trauma and then erase memories had a serious drawback, aside from the one-on-one experimentation, which interfered with the broader purpose of being able to control entire populations. It is the total memory loss that as always made me wonder what happened to me, as it has with many other people I have spoken with. There had to be a different way to control the mind and it was found in the work of Nicolai Tesla and Albert Einstein.

I believe that the energy control aspect of these programs has not yet been written about or revealed, a variation of MKUltra that involves the manipulation of human energy fields, something that Tesla and Einstein postulated about and quantum physics has vaguely defined as the collective consciousness. This energy field is the holy grail of mind control, and this derivation of the overall human control agenda wanted to harness the ability to control the energy from which human thought, emotion, and action are derived, that invisible quality which is the spark of life.

Did the mind control experiments discover a subgroup of victims who possessed a unique energetic imprint that presented a new frontier in human energy control? There are several different ways to look at this, including the alien presence from the 1940s and the technology/testing exchange agreements, which opened a new possibility for an even greater form of human control that would allow them to bypass trying to manipulate individual minds and instead, use energy as an invisible tool to control entire populations. If we look at the sublayers of energy control technologies in use today, such as GWEN and HAARP, as well as patents for similar products, this may be true.

These energy control experiments happened at the same time as the mind control programs, and may have been conducted on a smaller scale because the subjects were not from the general population, as were the more generalized mind control experimentation subjects. The energy control subjects were specifically selected for their intuitive abilities, energy frequency and sensitivity, intellectual aptitude, and empathy. This is what happened to me, and it happened to a lot of other people of my generation.

I believe that in addition to MKUltra and its misguided, unethical efforts at mind control, governments and scientists were trying to capture psychic energy to use in mass population manipulation and control. Russian scientists had been studying this topic for many years and had been using remote viewers, as had the Americans, to spy on other countries for decades. The Nazis were also known to be fascinated with psychic abilities, dark magic, Egyptian rites, sorcery, intuition, and other psycho-spiritual practices. Josef Mengele, the sinister architect of mind control experiments, had a fascination with twins and used them in many experiments to study the subtle interactions between them which were made possible by their unique connection and similarities. He was one of the many scientists who were brought to the United States after the war, via Operation Paperclip, given new identities and lives, and allowed to continue their gruesome experiments.

And their efforts were well timed because starting in the 1940s, a population of highly intuitive, energetically sensitive, empathic, psychic children was born, who had the energetic and psychic abilities they wanted to use, if they could figure out how to harness and manipulate their energy.

Although highly intuitive children have been around for centuries, the generation born starting in the 1940s represented a concentration of high energy and highly developed intuition that had never been seen before. If the governments could harness these children's energy, not only would they be able to influence vast populations' behavior and control the human energy field, which was their objective, they could also control the next wave of highly intuitive children, who would be born in the late 1950s and 1960s.

Now in order to fully understand the objectives of energy control experiments we have to consider that governments did not come up with this idea themselves, they were working with someone or something who knew about energy and who understood the significance and importance of the human energy's power and potential.

Who were these people?

It has been written that there was an alien invasion in the world in the 1940s and permission was granted to conduct experiments on humans in exchange for advanced alien technology. Whether you believe that is true or not, if we look at the methodologies and timelines for mind and energy control, they were initiated at a critical juncture in human energetic evolution.

To fully understand why these experiments on energy and mind control were conducted, and this is not even consider-ing the fields of human genetic experimentation, cloning, and other experimentation that we don't know much about, we have to go beyond the reasoning of general social deviance and sadism as the basis for these activities.

Is it possible that an alien planetary presence needed access to humans for their own ulterior purposes? Is it possible that the source of and reasons for energy and mind control is far broader than we can imagine? Despite vehement denial by the US government, which always means that they are lying about the truth, something happened at Roswell, New Mexico in July 1947, which was not to be shared with the general public or with the world, at all costs. And mind and energy control experimentation began in earnest at the same time as the denied UFO incident at Roswell.

Is this a coincidence? I don't think so and I don't believe in coincidences.

No matter how outlandish you think this may be, it's time for us to consider this as an alternate and reasonable truth because only by expanding into a broader range of possibilities for mind and energy control and embracing a new truth, that other types of non-human beings live among us, can we connect all of the dots and explain the mystery of mind and energy control technology and why it is being done at all, and why it merits so much time, money, and attention.

Accepting this alien presence, that probably began before July 1947, is the only way to explain the exponential advances in technology that began in the early 1950s. How did we suddenly invent television, advanced weapons technology, radar, supersonic travel, and computers? Although early technology looks ridiculous today, if you consider that prior to the 1950s none of it existed, and that technology has grown exponentially every year since then, some outside assistance and information have been provided to make this possible.

Harry Truman jokingly referred to having meetings with aliens but I don't think he was joking. He was telling the truth, although at the time no one would have believed him. And the presence of aliens was a closely guarded secret, administered by secret government agencies with access denied to all but a select few, which supposedly did not include the U.S. president. What was so important about this that it had to be hidden from everyone?

One thing that's true about governments, they only hide the 'good stuff', so whatever happened involving aliens during WWII or after Roswell, the information was so important and so powerful that someone wanted to keep away from everyone else.

And it was in 1947 that the National Security Act was passed, which provided the legal justification for mind control experimentation to gain momentum. Since then mind and energy control programs have been funded to the tune of hundreds of billions, even trillions of dollars with experiments conducted in the United States, Canada, the United Kingdom, and other countries around the world. If the mind can be controlled, then the mind's creative ability can also be manipulated. I believe that while the initial focus was on mind control, the real desire was to learn how to control human energy, that creative spirit that is what makes us unique in the universe.

But we have to wonder what was so special about this energy that they would go to so much time and expense to control it?

Why were they doing these experiments in the first place and who, or what, was the driving force behind them?

I'll leave that up to your imagination but the reasons are highly suspicious since they coincide with the Roswell alien presence in 1947, and the race to control the human mind and energy began after that date. I believe that this alien presence needed access to human energy and that is why they were here on earth. And they traded their highly advanced technology for access to humans for experimentation, something which has been reported by others for decades.

The new generations of highly sensitive, intuitive, empathic children had a high degree of compassion, kindness, integrity, love, and awareness. These future world citizens and leaders would have no interest in war, control, domination, or manipulation. They would do away with the elitist, monopolistic, corporate culture that has dominated the world and that energy needed to be controlled because it meant the demise of those whose focus was absolute, unchallenged control of populations for their own benefit.

They would have no interest in partnering with non-human groups or elements who wanted to harness human energy. In fact, their higher energy would make it impossible for these alien, or non-human elements, unless they were peaceful, compassionate, and loving, to exist on the planet. To prevent this from happening and to control these children they would have to learn how to harness and manipulate their energy. And since their energy was 'natural', and not artificial or man-made, it was believed that the ability to use a natural human energy source would be superior to using artificial energy created by machines or transmitters.

And so the ultra secret energy control program was born. The experiments were kept secret for obvious reasons -- how would the government explain that they were expanding Nazi-era experiments to further develop and refine ways to create 'super humans' who could be used as weapons against each other, and to control and manipulate the energy of their people at will? Even in the 1950s people would have had a problem with that, as they do today.

I'll refer to my own experiences here but I have also shared some of this information and some of my insights with many thousands of people in my social media communities and the responses were disturbing. Many people, many of them part of the intuitive, sensitive generation born between the 1940s and 1980s, also remembered being hospitalized as young children, they also had big gaps in their childhood memory, were tested in school and spent time with psychoanalysts and psychologists, and they had irrational and unexplainable fears as children and as adults too, stemming from things they could not remember.

Many of them, like me, had a father who was in government service or in the military. At a time when authority was not questioned, it was easy to convince parents that their children were being taken for simple observation, for obscure reasons that did not require unnecessary explanations. After all, governments took care of their citizens, they didn't abuse, manipulate, or lie to them.

At a time when social approval and appearances were so important, it was also easy for a government or military to coerce, blackmail, or manipulate a parent into agreeing to secret testing of their children to protect a job, career, or reputation.

That's why MKUltra was able to continue for as long as it did, because no one questioned it. We question it now because too many people have stepped forward with stories of their horrible experiences in hospitals and secret laboratories. And don't be fooled by assertions that the mind control research programs ended, they continue to this day and have even been expanded to include higher level energy control technologies that include human cloning, genetic manipulation, advanced energy technology and psychotronic and psychotropic tools, powerful mind controlling drugs, human drones, neural networks, and advanced artificial intelligence.

But our awareness has limited these programs' effectiveness as far as mass population control is concerned, and our knowledge of the secret human energy experiment programs, will render them even more ineffective. Once we know about these efforts at controlling and manipulating our energy, they lose their effectiveness and their power is vastly reduced. Once we can name something or know its true purpose, we can no longer fear it or be controlled by it.

How do you know if this happened to you? This is a list of some of the general effects and situations reported and experienced by me and others involved in human mind and energy control experiments. You may have some or many of these but if you have the slightest suspicion that you were a victim of human energy control experimentation, then you probably were.

Mind/Energy Control Symptoms List

You were born between 1940 and 1980

You were an intuitive, sensitive, empathic, or psychic child

You had a parent in the military or in government service

You spent time in a military hospital, or in a large civilian hospital as a child, and you may not be able to remember your experiences

You have blanks in your childhood memory, periods that you cannot remember anything about

You are not in family photos for a period of time or your parents have 'lost' or misplaced photos of you

You have strong fears of being isolated, abandoned or abused and still have them today

You have a vague memory of sexual and/or physical abuse

You have strong feelings of shame and a fear of humiliation

You are prone to addictive behavior, such as OCD, or have a strong need to be in control of your environment

You feel that you were not raised in the same way as your siblings

You either have substance abuse problems, drugs or alcohol, or you are strongly against them and do not take drugs or drink

You know that you were separated from your parents for periods of time during your childhood,

You were given IQ and other tests in schools and were singled out for your high test scores

You were taken out of your regular school classes and talked to counselors or were given tests that the other children in your classes were not given

You have irrational fears about being attacked or hurt by someone

You are afraid of the dark, closed spaces, and you are mildly or severely claustrophobic

You do not like being cold and always have a sweater or jacket with you

If you are a parent, you are very protective of your children and are afraid that they will be sexually abused or that something will happen to them

You are afraid of needles and of receiving shots

You are mildly or severely depressed, have suicidal thoughts, feel hopeless at times, and have moderate to severe mood swings that you cannot control

You have had a severe or life threatening health issue since 2007

You feel stuck and unmotivated, have a strong fear of being in the public eye, or of being 'seen' or noticed, and while you may have dreams of success, you cannot make them a reality

You feel a deep sadness at times and feel grief over something you feel you have lost, but you do not know what it is

At different times in your life, you have felt completely unable to act or to take action, even if it was necessary to maintain your physical, financial, or emotional well-being

You can remember being very angry with your parents as a child

You choose friends and romantic partners who do not meet your needs, or who take advantage of you

You have been married at least twice or several times and your relationships tend to be dysfunctional

You had one or more abortions as a young adult

You have financial issues and don't know how to make or handle money

You have had moderate to severe, short to long term memory blackouts as an adult, especially in your 20s and 30s or especially in the 1980s to around 2010

You know something has happened to you, but you have no idea what it is.

These are some of the aspects that I have identified from what has happened to me, as well as what has been shared with me by others. This is just the tip of the iceberg, so to speak. As we learn more about these programs and the concept of human energy control, and this knowledge will come from others who share their stories because the government certainly isn't going to own up to it, we add to this list to understand the full implication of these experiences. Then we will know and understand the cause of our pain, sadness, and fear, and release it to regain our memories and control of our energy.

WHAT WE NEED TO KNOW ABOUT MIND AND ENERGY CONTROL

Sensory deprivation, psychological manipulation, mind controlling drugs, sexual abuse and sexual torture, including rape, are all part of the MKUltra mind control toolkit, as they create severe emotional and psychic trauma in their victims. And in highly sensitive, intuitive, and empathic children, the level of trauma is exponentially amplified, and it lowers their energy frequency which makes it easier to manipulate and harness their energy. These are among the many methods used in energy control programs too, along with psychotropic drugs to create memory blackouts, and other drugs that are used to maintain post-trauma hypnotic suggestive states.

As I mentioned earlier, the results of the mind control programs that were begun by the Nazis in WWII internment camps were eagerly pounced upon by the military, government, scientists, and researchers after the war. While a few scapegoats were tried for war crimes, over one thousand Nazis, researchers, scientists, doctors, and thought leaders, and all of their research and test results were secretly brought to the United States to continue their work. At taxpayer expense they were provided with new identities and financial support to continue and expand their experiments in mind control.

The Nazi architect of many of these experiments, Dr. Josef Mengele, who conducted barbaric experiments on Jews in the Auschwitz Nazi concentration camp, was provided safe haven to the U.S., where he became known as 'Dr. Brown', instead of being prosecuted for war crimes or fleeing from the allies, as has been reported. Many of the MKUltra mind control experiment practices and methods are based on his work, especially those involving sensory deprivation, torture, and abuse.

While the mind control portion of these experiments is widely known, as well as their modern day counterparts, Monarch and Beta Programming, which have infiltrated the entertainment industry, television, print, music, art, and nearly every aspect of life today, very little is known about the human energy control program. But I know that it's very real. And it's affecting all of us today, especially the technology that has been developed with the human energy control experiments.

Why was this done, what was its objective, and why is it continuing?

To get to the truth requires an intellectual stretch because we can't talk about mind and energy control, mass manipulation, and secret government programs, which are already unbelievable enough and that's just considering the ones we do know about, without addressing topics that few people can believe, much less acknowledge could be part of our daily lives, energy, non-human beings or aliens, and governments that plot against their citizens.

And of course we have to consider that maybe those who have been talking about this for decades, that everyone calls 'crazy conspiracy theorists', may have been right about many things. The fact is, they were right and what we know today is just the tip of a very big, mean, and dangerous iceberg. But like all icebergs, it can be melted and that's what we're going to do, together.

We also cannot really answer the question of 'why' this is being done because there is no answer that will satisfy us, the 'normal' people. Why would anyone want to program someone's mind so they drive a car into a crowd of people, or pick up a gun and started shooting at the people around them, or decide to rob a bank and take hostages, or drown their children? If you recognize any similar current events here, it's because all of those have been actual events that were done by real people.

But those people were not mentally ill or unstable, as was reported by the media. Instead, they were victims of mind control experiments, dosed with powerful psychotropic drugs, traumatized in mind control exercises, and then controlled via post-trauma hypnotic suggestions that allowed them to become tools for mind control technology in the form of energy control.

And they were all, for a few moments, completely 'out of their minds' because something had taken over their minds and thought processes. They cannot really be charged for these crimes because while their bodies may have been involved in the acts, whatever energy controlling their minds was not their own.

What's the point of mind control? Controlling people so that they commit acts of violence or chaos that inspire fear and disrupt social order. One person who commits a highly public, fearsome act can create fear in a lot of people. Then maybe a zombie race is created, where everyone is mind controlled and they all kill and maim each other. If it sounds like something out of a horror movie, it isn't, this is a real life scenario. This technology exists and it's being used on us right now. You'll read about it in the next chapter.

But don't get too worried because although it is designed to work in a specific way, it has important limitations that severely restrict its ability to impact a lot of people. And the more we understand and know about human energy control and mind control technologies, the more power and control we have over them so they don't work on anyone. And we can make that happen when we work together and understand our energy.

THE METHODOLOGY – THE WHY
AND HOW OF ENERGY CONTROL

To understand the purpose and methodology of energy control we have to consider that we have been lied to about nearly everything we accept as truth today, especially UFOs, alien technology, human psychobiology, and the existence of a collective energetic super-consciousness. If you can accept that and understand that there is a secret war being fought for control of humanity's energy, then this next part will make a lot of sense to you.

As humans we are the most creative force in the universe, and we have particular abilities that make us unique among other types of beings, our ability to use and control energy. If you have ever wished for something and it happened, or you think about someone and they call you, this is what the human creative ability to focus energy is all about. In the past ten years many experiments involving focused thought and intention, such as global meditation experiments, have shown amazing results.

A group of people, large or small, who agree to focus their energy on peace, love, joy, healing, or other positive intentions, create measurable shifts in energetic frequency in the collective energy field. Scientists have observed sympathetic action among protons, where an action done to one is responded to by the other, even when they are thousands of miles apart. Imagine the changes that could occur if all of humanity was using their energy to create peace in the world -- war would cease to exist.

But there is a group that doesn't want this to happen, which includes the leaders of post WWII governments, including their secret or shadow counterparts. Their life force and power relies on the presence of fear and the only reason they can exist on the planet is that there are people who are willing to engage in the energy of fear, to hate, to engage in violence, to fight, and to want to control and dominate others.

This is the energy frequency they need, and it is the only way they can sustain themselves on our planet. Once there are no more people who are willing to hate their fellow humans or fear can no longer be used to control humanity, they will no longer have any power because they feed on the energy of fear and without fear energy they cannot exist.

Since we have free will we can use our energy in any way we choose. And whether we use it or not, we have access to all of our energy, at any frequency we choose to be at. But if we have been the victim of human energy control experiments and if we are not using our energy with intentional awareness, or are unaware that we have an energy field and are energetic beings, then our energy can be manipulated by anyone who knows how or who has set up systems to allow that to happen.

Human energy is manipulated and controlled through fear and emotional trauma. Whether that's watching a violent television show, or listening to hate-filled music lyrics, or being inundated by endless news reports by talking heads about another mass 'shooting' by an allegedly psychotic person, or a significant weather event, the real purpose behind all of these incidents is to generate fear and to control energy frequency in the mass population. This is not a new science, these types of experiments have been going on for a long time.

For example, in the 1960s subliminal advertising was all the rage, until it was revealed that advertisers were using secretly embedded images and messages to control and manipulate their audiences' feelings and emotions about their products. There was the predictable public outrage, apologies by advertising agencies, a token government inquiry, and then the practice was supposedly stopped. But it wasn't   and the effectiveness of subliminal advertising became a fertile proving ground for the evolution of human energy and mind control methodologies.

Fear is the objective of all control-based programming and experimentation, and its results are obtained through trauma, the more shocking and traumatic the better. The human energy field is very strong and resilient, but it fails in the face of trauma, especially when it's deliberate, ongoing, intentional, and is begun as early in life as possible. Once a human is highly traumatized, their energy field becomes malleable and controllable, and the fear engine has another source of energy.

The more fear that can be generated through these efforts, the more the fear machine gets fed. This is being done to the majority of the earth's population today, although many are wising up to this manipulation and are tuning it out. The efforts to incite fear and chaos are now so blatantly obvious that many people are beginning to question the truth of most of what they see and hear.

We now live in an era where 'crisis actor' is a new career path and shootings are Hollywood-style staged events, coordinated by movie producers, defense contractors, governments, and law enforcement agencies, accompanied by a group of well compensated actors who are paid to look injured or play dead, all in the name of generating fear energy.

If you have been a victim of human energy control experiments, you feel and are impacted by this mass energy control in subtle ways. While you may try to avoid the fear mongering by avoiding the media, you are manipulated in different ways, by implants, energy siphons, blocks, energy technology such as GWEN and HAARP, and by energy surrogates. These are all explained here, including how they work and how you can deactivate them or make yourself non-susceptible and put yourself out of their reach.

Do you think this is too far out to be believable? In the Resources section I have included a few articles I found, dating from the 1980s and 1990s, that describe 'human implant technology' and the first HAARP patent was filed in 1985. Nicolai Tesla filed a number of patents between the late 1800s and early 1900s that described the concept of energy control and today's energy control technology uses his work. Look at the descriptions for some of the patents named in this section, for devices that 'actively and passively track humans', or a 'silent subliminal presentation system'. It's scary stuff but it's real and that's what we need to focus on, the reality of the situation, so we can regain control of our energy. Also look up 'psychotronic weapons', technology that is used to control and even kill people through brain and energy manipulation.

One more thing we need to explore, and it's the most difficult topic to address, and that is the use of trauma in mind and energy control programming, especially physical and sexual torture and abuse, and why it is such an important aspect of this technology. In the next section, where I discuss the different types of human energy control technology and how they work, I reveal how this technology requires the disruption of and access points into the human energy field, which are created by trauma.

I have to say that of everything I know about this technology this is by far the most disgusting and evil aspect. Who would torture, abuse, rape, and torment anyone, especially an infant or a young child? It is a major component of energy and mind control technology because it is the only way to create a big enough disruption in the human energy field to allow insertion of lower frequency energy.

We have all had life situations that were traumatic and maybe some of you have been physically or sexually abused as children. The resulting psychic, psychological, and emotional damage takes years to recover from and full recovery never really happens. It stays with the victim as a dark memory, a dark spot in their psyche which creates a corresponding dark spot in their energy field.

This is what trauma does to us on an energy level and it is an access point for human energy control technology. The expansion of these dark spots in energy fields is the purpose of intentionally created fear events. But they work in the presence of fear and the absence of awareness. Introducing awareness opens the portal of understanding and recalibrates the energy field so that fear becomes ineffective, and attempts at mind and energy control cease to work.

People who have been traumatized suffer from Post Traumatic Stress Disorder, PTSD, and years later the memory of their trauma can be triggered by an event that sends them back into their traumatic state. For war veterans this can be loud noises, for a rape victim it can be meeting someone who resembles their attacker, for a mind control victim, it can be a pre-programmed key word or suggestion that was created during their programming or an event or situation that recalls their trauma or, as I have experienced, trying to access a forbidden or hidden memory.

The mind is capable of compartmentalization, where it creates a boundary between our daily conscious thinking and the trauma that is too painful for us to think about or remember so we can avoid thinking about it. The trauma is not forgotten though, it is pushed far back into the memory so it cannot be easily or readily accessed. But it's still there and when a triggering event occurs it is immediately recalled to the present, as though the trauma was happening at that moment.

And here is another aspect of the mind's functionality that makes mind and energy control effective. The mind has no concept of time and doesn't delegate memory or emotional response based on how long ago something happened. If your fear was created by an event that happened ten years ago, you will be just as afraid if you face that situation today as you were ten years ago. It's part of the mind's protective systems, and it is what is used to manipulate and control human mind and energy control victims. The human energy control programming relies on the presence of this traumatic state that it uses to gain access into the human energy field.

The kind of trauma created in human mind and energy control programming ranges from moderate to severe and that involves physical, mental, emotional, psychic, and sexual abuse on every level. While the horrific abuse is at one end of the spectrum, the more benign abuse is equally damaging although it appears to be negligible.

Think about how much more violent TV shows and movies are now than they were twenty years ago. How much more violent are music lyrics and what has happened to the music we could sing along with? Look at today's stage performances and music videos too, which are full of strange occult symbols, strong sexual references, and odd behavior.

While these may appear to be unimportant in reality they are very significant because they are part of energy control technology protocols, designed for the gradual desensitization to violent behavior, to traumatize people in slow, measured doses, and to create outrage, anger, and fear at the same time, which creates confusion at an energetic level, but all within the same energy frequency spectrum. It's all part of the overall master plan of energy control and that's the more benign form.

There is a far more serious aspect, and that is the one designed to create energy tools out of humans, to deliberately destroy their self awareness and create human robots that can follow orders without question. And you do not have to look far to see them, as there are prime examples within the most highly celebrated members of the entertainment industry and they have all been subjected to mind and energy control program-ming.

The other end of the energy and mind control abuse spectrum is the full scale assault on the human spirit. These assaults are designed to subject the child or adult victim to the most violent and severe forms of abuse and trauma, to subject them to their most powerful fears, including death, abandonment, and isolation. The victim believes it is going to be killed and is it at the mercy of its abuser. The trauma is systematic, planned, usually by trained psychologists and psychiatrists, and carefully orchestrated so that the victim is pulled from the brink of death or exhaustion by its attacker, creating the belief that is has been rescued and this also creates a false attachment to its rescuer. The abuser then becomes the savior and a mind and energy control threshold has been achieved.

Or there is systematic abuse designed to dominate, control, humiliate, shock, or bring the victim to an acute stage of terror, then the conscious memory is wiped away through a combination of post-trauma hypnotic suggestion and drugs, but the terror and its energy remains and the victim's energy field contains a powerful entry point for future manipulation and control.

But there is a middle ground in this process, one that is more subtle in nature. 'Terrorism' is the new global mind control tool as we are protected from alleged terrorist attacks, which occur with singularly curious regularity. Then our governments rush in with new levels of security and protection, to save us from a far harsher reality.

When the abuse is a one-time event, the mind can compartmentalize its trauma, to put it away and to protect itself by keeping it out of its daily conscious memory. It is still a traumatic event but it can be dealt with and over time, the memory fades.

But when the abuse is deliberate and ongoing, begins in infancy, or on a regular basis, and is augmented by drugs, hypnosis, and intentional and systematic reinforcement, the mind further compartmentalizes the trauma by splitting its personality into different aspects in order to deal with the abuse.

It puts up a false front or persona, so that the abuse is not happening to 'it', it is happening to someone else. This is what psychologists call disassociation and it is a dangerous mind state that can give birth to psychopathic personality types as the victim's connection to any type of compassion or empathy is removed.

The MKUltra mind programming protocol uses this type of trauma conditioning to create human assassins, people who can kill with impunity because they have no ability to empathize or feel compassion for their victims, or for anyone else, including themselves. Ted Bundy, Charles Manson, Timothy McVeigh, David Berkowitz, the Columbine School Shooters, Mark David Chapman (John Lennon's killer) are all victims of MKUltra mind programming and are all human assassins. This is not a comprehensive list of human assassins but one notable fact is that many people who can be placed in this category have spent time in military service and most, if not all, have also spent time in psychiatric hospitals or institutions.

Over time and in the presence of constant trauma the energy field begins to fracture, to scatter and distance itself from the trauma that is happening to the physical body. As the energy field loses its integrity it also becomes porous, in a way that creates openings or access points for other energies to enter. While the human psyche is strong, there is only so much abuse and fear that we can tolerate and when we begin to lose hope in the face of unrelenting abuse, fear, terror, and trauma, we do our best to remove ourselves from what is causing us pain. This makes us perfect targets for human energy control implants, suggestions, and programming.

Before you think that this type of energetic fracturing and abuse only occurs within laboratories and hospitals, and is only relegated to the helpless victims of mad scientists funded by the CIA and various demented governments, think again. The constant pressure of a life lived on the edge of financial disaster, the threat of homelessness, the specter of poor health, the fear of global annihilation, the belief that we are surrounded by wild terrorists whose only objective is to kill us all, all of these create the same kind of mental torment and energetic fracturing as some of the more severe human energy and mind control experimentation.

And male infants experience their first trauma within hours after birth, when they are circumcised. This is a completely unnecessary and arbitrary procedure that is foisted on every male child born today, especially in the United States. Parents are bullied into having their male children circumcised, which is a Jewish religious practice, whether they want it or not, or follow the Jewish religion or not. It is medically unnecessary, except in very rare cases, and is dangerous to children as it is highly traumatic, and circumcisions are generally performed with no anesthesia. For decades doctors insisted that infants did not feel pain which is complete nonsense. But performing this surgery so soon after birth creates an energetic disruption that is extremely harmful to children and represents their first life trauma.

Given what I now know about human energy control programs and experiments, I have to question whether the medical community's insistence on the value of male infant circumcision is connected to human energy control programming, as the medical, psychological, and psychiatric associations in the US and in the global community were and are still heavily implicated in MKUltra testing. And generalized male circumcision was implemented in the 1950s, at the zenith of MKUltra mind control testing and experimentation. You can put the pieces together and see whether there are any connections to be made. As I said before, there are no coincidences, especially when we're dealing with secret mind control experimentation.

Decades of overt and covert human mind and energy control programming and experimentation have created a subculture of humans who are highly susceptible to energetic manipulation. And the technology used to manipulate them is in place and is being used today. We need this information now because if we're going to overcome the programming and manipulation, which we can do, we need to know what we're dealing with.

As you read about energy implants, blocks, siphons, suggestions, and surrogates, remember that all of them very real and are in use now. Pay attention to the ones that you have the strongest reaction to, as they may be the ones you have personal experience with. And keep reading because in the section after that, I explain how to de-activate, disarm, destroy, and release yourself from the effects of this technology.

First, I want to talk about how the military has been a testing ground for mind control and energy control technology for nearly one hundred years. And in particular, a mind control experiment that went wrong in the early days of mind control experimentation, or right, depending on which side you were on, the scientists who programmed the test subjects or the victims of their human assassins.

THE MILITARY & THE MURDER OF MARTIN DRENOVAC

On June 8, 1961, Martin Drenovac, a gas station and restaurant owner in Illinois, was murdered by two men after he serviced their car. He was their fifth victim in a two week killing spree that involved seven murders, six car jackings, and multiple assaults. George York and Ronald Latham, the two men who killed Drenovac, were identified as soldiers who were away without leave from their posts at the military base in Fort Hood, Texas. They were also described as racists who hated the world, were angry at the lack of segregation in their barracks, and were known to often leave the base without permission. Their killing spree ended with a standoff in Utah and they were later hanged in Kansas, after a jury refused to consider an insanity plea as their defense.

The law enforcement officers who were present at their arrest were shocked that the two showed an extreme level of callous indifference towards their actions and displayed no remorse whatsoever. They could not understand how two people could cause so much mayhem and then joke about it.

Instead, the pair bragged about the number of people they had assaulted and killed, obviously disappointed that two people had survived their shootings. Psychiatrists who examined them decided that they exhibited passive-aggressive behavior and thought York was a 'paranoid sociopath' while Latham was a 'schizoid sociopath'. The two were sentenced to death row and were hanged in 1965. Truman Capote based his book, *In Cold Blood,* on them.

But disturbing details emerge if we look more closely at York and Latham. James Latham received his military basic training in Fort Carson, Colorado, home of the secret National Reconnaissance Project, whose mission is to maintain security on all alien-related spacecraft and is a known mind and energy control experimentation super site. And both men were stationed at Fort Bliss, Texas, another site of extensive secret mind control experimentation and the MK-Delta program.

In 1960, the CIA introduced its MK-Delta program, (MK identifies this program as a subset of the Mind Kontrol group of programs) designed to perfect existing electromagnetic energy control technology using a range of frequencies from VHF (Very High Frequency) to ELF (Extremely Low Frequencies). The purpose of these experiments that used an array of different levels of energy frequencies on their test subjects, was to induce fatigue, mood swings, behavior dysfunction, and socially criminal behavior.

The purpose of the MK-Delta program was to create a population of engineered killers, super-soldiers who would kill on command and follow deadly force orders against their own friends, neighbors, and fellow citizens, without question or hesitation, showing no remorse, compassion, or emotion.

York and Latham were already social misfits when they entered the army. They were angry racists who generally blamed the world for their problems and that made them prime test subjects for the MK-Delta program which used their own anger-based negative energy levels to turn them into callous killers.

The use of low frequency energy on people who are naturally in a low frequency range would effectively suppress any natural ability to express compassion or remorse, as well as expanding their already high levels of negative energy. The effect would be like putting gasoline on a raging bonfire. The CIA's MK-Delta program was designed to create human assassins and once they had adequately prepared York and Latham to fulfill this objective, they set them loose to see what would happen.

Their killing spree was no accident, it was a carefully conducted experiment to see how the human energy control assassin technology would function in the general population. York and Latham were not operating in a war zone, they were in cities and towns, driving around the countryside, stealing cars and attacking people. They assaulted normal, ordinary people who were going about their daily lives, and who had the misfortune to cross paths with these two men who were programmed to kill indiscriminately.

And the experiment was a resounding success with one tiny flaw, the killers had no 'kill switch'. Once the killers were released into the general population, they could not be stopped. Once their killing orders had been issued, they would kill indiscriminately until they were destroyed using the same type of deadly force they wantonly used on their victims. Activating the 'killer instinct' required that all energy that would lessen or mitigate that instinct be removed from the killer's emotional processing system, so once a killer or a super soldier assassin was created, destroying it permanently was the only way to stop it.

Deliberately crafted stories about York and Latham were released to the media, blaming the men, their upbringing, their general shiftlessness, racism, and anger as the reasons behind their crimes, but the truth is they had no control over what they were doing and in some ways were as innocent of their crimes as the victims they murdered. They had been carefully programmed to do exactly what they did and once that energy control technology was activated within them, they were completely beyond anyone's control, even that of their programmers.

If anyone is to blame for the deaths of Martin Drenovac and Latham and York's other innocent victims, it is the military in conjunction with the CIA and the entire mind and energy control protocol establishment.

Energy control technology was advancing at a furious pace in the 1960s, and what we call HAARP and GWEN today has its roots in those early experiments on the use of energy to control human thought and behavior. Military personnel and their families provided easy access to a population of test subjects, and soldiers, sailors, airmen, and marines have been the unwitting victims of mind and energy control testing for over fifty years.

Since 2000, the pace of this testing has increased dramatically and the military has pursued a policy of collaboration and collusion with the scientific and corporate communities to not only allow this testing to occur, but has made its personnel available for experimentation and has sanctioned it at all levels of military service. How many veterans return from war with unexplained physical and emotional problems?

Why are their symptoms and conditions denounced or denied, and why they are not offered treatment? It's sadly true that this isn't part of the program.

Is it possible that once mind control mechanisms are in place that they cannot be deactivated? They can, but not by the people who caused the problem in the first place. They don't have the levels of empathy, compassion, or awareness to undo their work and they don't want to. The 'kill switch' for human energy control protocols is not part of these programs. Their engineers and architects want to dominate and control populations and that is their agenda, goal, intention, and purpose. Caring about the consequences to their test subjects and victims is beyond the scope of their own energetic abilities. To be honest, they exhibit the same levels of negative energy as York and Latham, 'cold blooded killers' with a power-mad agenda.

The proof of mind and energy control is undeniable and we have been provided with many clues as to how this is happening via the film industry, which is itself a tool of the mind and energy control establishment, and has quietly injected evidence of these efforts in many movies. I already mentioned the *Hearts in Atlantis* movie, but there are many others. MacGyver's Season 2, Episode 16 entitled *Brainwashed* , which aired live on April 24, 1989, describes the training and use of mind controlled assassins. I remember seeing that episode when it aired live in 1989 but I thought it was just a dramatic make-believe movie concept. At that time, the idea that this could happen in real life wasn't even on my radar, nor was it on any-one else's. It was just the work of a creative screenwriter, pure science fiction.

In the TV series 'The 4400' which aired from 2004 to 2007, a 'super soldier program' is described and members of the cast are attacked by a group of these soldiers who have remarkable extra-sensory and physical abilities, who simply follow orders and kill with impunity. Popular science fiction shows like Star Trek, Stargate, and others also feature the use of mind and energy control, and all of them aired live at a time when this technology was being heavily tested on the general population. These are a few examples, you can find your own if you look for them.

We may be inclined to believe that this is Hollywood make-believe but it is the truth that is stranger than fiction. This stuff goes on every day and, as you will read in a later chapter, it is being used on populations around the world, and especially in the US, Canada, and the UK, on a continuous basis.

Are military personnel being turned into a deadly killing machine? That is the ultimate result that the military, the CIA, the secret government agencies, and mind/energy control establishment would like to see but these results are not forthcoming. Instead, they are seeing a record number of suicides among active duty and personnel who return from battle zones and while they try to create a body of possible reasons for it, this is a result of mind and energy control technology gone wrong.

A January 2015 Los Angeles Times article reports that suicide among veterans who have served in wars since 2000 has reach alarming levels and is significantly higher than that of the non-military population. This statistic is noteworthy because it represents a total reversal from veteran suicide rates in pre-2000 wars, which were typically significantly less than the general population. Men are three times more likely to kill themselves than women, veteran suicide is more likely to happen within three years after leaving active duty, and the suicide rate for female veterans is double that of the general female non-military population.

What is going on here?

A combination of mind and energy control programming is being both tested and used on service men and women every day, especially those in active duty military situations. The lack of independent oversight on the battlefields of Iraq and Afghanistan, and other far flung places make them an ideal environment to test and implement mind and energy control with impunity. The soldiers don't know what is happening to them, their families are too far away to notice and intervene, and it is all shrouded in the enforced secrecy demanded by anti-terrorism measures and national security.

From mind controlling drugs to performance enhancing chemicals, to the use of subliminal low energy frequencies and suggestions, to the continuous trauma of being in a dangerous battle situation, these men and women are being groomed using mind control technology methods, to become 'super soldiers' who can, after they complete their military service, be trained to kill on command and without question, with impunity and without remorse, like Latham and York.

The purpose of this extension and expansion of the CIA's ML-Delta program is to create an army of human assassins that will do things that normal soldiers will not do. If the government decides to impose martial law, put the military in charge of our cities and towns, and get rid of any dissenting voices, they know that convincing soldiers to use lethal force on their family and friends would be impossible. But if those same soldiers have been trained as assassins and will obey kill orders unquestioningly, they will fire upon anyone they are told to and can easily exterminate populations at will, without remorse, conscience, or compassion because those responses and emotions have been cut out of their mind's processing through a combination of abuse, deprivation, fear, drugs, trauma conditioning, and energy control.

If this is true, why are so many soldiers and veterans committing suicide now? Because many things have changed in the 55 years since Latham and York went on their killing spree. We are no longer a nation of misfits and racists, our new social order is built on connection, social media, accessibility, and the removal of social, cultural, and geographic boundaries. Men now push their babies in their strollers, carry diaper bags, and change diapers. Manliness is no longer defined by insensitivity, emotional distance, and indifference to compassion and empathy.

Resonance, alignment, and emotional intelligence are part of our everyday language. We have a reverence for life, connection, for our planet, and for each other. Power currency is taking a back seat to social currency and no one is interested in the power, control, and domination activities that pit us against each other while banks and armies sit on the sidelines, watching us fight their battles while they count their profits. And thanks to the constant availability of social media, we are also more connected to each other than ever before. As a global community, we now at a much higher collective energy frequency, one that is not easily controlled or manipulated.

When active duty soldiers return home they are removed from the relentless levels of energy control that they experience in the highly managed and controlled environments found on military bases, either domestic or international. They also go back to the places where they are loved and feel connected to, and these emotions quickly take over to undo their energy and mind control programming, no matter how strong it is.

Then, when they feel their mind control programming being activated and they are given orders to hurt, abuse, or kill someone, they cannot do it and, unable to resist the urge to harm others, they kill themselves instead. This isn't a far flung theory or a theme from a movie. Look at how many of the armed forces personnel who commit suicide are Marines, or soldiers who are in special forces or battle units, those who have specialized combat training, or who have been deployed in battle multiple times.

While the armed forces likes to pin the blame on combat fatigue and PTSD, the truth is the combination of active duty stress plus all of the mind and energy control use and experimentation that is happening to these soldiers is rearranging their body's energy systems so they can no longer control their thinking or their actions.

But the energy control technology is limited to use on a specific human energy frequency range, similar to that of York and Latham. As long as we keep our energy high, we will feel energy control technology as annoying or uncomfortable, or not at all. And no matter how much they try, it has become impossible to keep ahead of the current pace of human energetic evolution, a pace that I am proud to say that as the leading voice in the self-awareness movement and the world's only energy savante I have played an active part in this movement since 1991.

If you think this is scary stuff, it is. But as devious, dire, and demented as it is, it is no match for the power of the human spirit once it awakens into awareness. No matter how strong energy technology becomes, as long as we remain aligned with our highest possible energy frequencies and remain aware of the attempts to lower our energy frequencies, which will continue in the near to long term, we will be fine.

Now, if you want to find out what all of the fuss is about, what energy control technology is, how it works, and how you can manage it in your own life, read on. There are also some resources for reading at the end of this book, as well as on the book website humanenergycontrolbook.com.

HUMAN ENERGY CONTROL METHODS

Human energy control technology exists in the form of a variety of tools that act as energy receivers, amplifiers, and transmitters, some are actual physical implants, others involve energetic manipulation, some function in conjunction with psychotropic and mind altering drugs, others work through a combination of all of these and through post trauma hypnotic suggestion.

Physical implants range in size from those described as 'large', which are about the size of the head of a ballpoint pen, to nano-sized, small enough to be inserted at the cellular level. They are introduced into the body via vaccines, injections, or surgery and can also be introduced via food and airborne methods, such as the chemicals and other elements dumped into the atmosphere via chemtrails. The metallic composition of some of the chemtrail elements are designed to work in conjunction with the ELF (Extremely Low Frequency) and other high density, low vibration technologies.

They work with radio waves, infrared, high definition, ultra sound, laser, audio, or microwave technology. In 2009 the

US government mandated the switch from analog to digital broadcasting via federal law. High definition television, which was first introduced in 1998, has become the new standard for TV. While it does deliver a better picture and has made televisions more portable, why was it necessary to turn off analog broadcasting, and to pass a federal law to that effect, with a stringent deadline, which was enforced at the highest levels of government?

Because HDTV and digital broadcasting allows the dissemination of a variety of levels of energy control technologies directly into people's homes. And they work with GWEN towers and HAARP technology, to maintain a continuous flow of energetic frequencies that are programmed to coincide with different types of broadcasts. At the time the federal law for digital broadcasting was passed, which I thought was highly suspicious, I thought it was extreme on the part of the government and wondered what kind of collusion was happening between them and the cable companies. There was collusion, but it wasn't with the cable companies, it was with the mind and energy control establishment.

With HDTV as the new national standard, high definition energy waves could reach every household and a new level of energy control deliver was in place. I am conjecturing here, but I do believe that when there is some kind of fear based, negative TV programming, like a 'terrorist' attack, a shooting, destructive weather, or some other event that can be used to augment fear in people, the TV programming and the high definition energy frequencies are correlated , so the greatest fear response can be created.

This is subliminal advertising on steroids, the kind of audience influencing technology used in the 1960s, but that arrives as a silent messenger, through television and the radio. Listen to the famous 1960s Simon and Garfunkel hit 'The Sounds of Silence' because they describe an energy control technology initially developed in the 1950s called Silent Sound Spread Spectrum, or SSSS, or, as the military calls it, 'S-quad'. It is so powerful that, when it was used on Saddam Hussein's elite military troops, they all surrendered without firing a single shot.

SSSS technology connects directly with the mind, manipulating the brain's energy patterns and altering its energy state. It is capable of implanting any kind of emotional state, usually negative, like fear anxiety, despair, powerlessness, depression, and hopelessness, directly into the mind. Because it works at the brain level, the victim thinks it is coming from them but it isn't, it is the SSSS technology that is altering their brain state. And this technology needs HDTV to act as a receiver and transmitter, which is why the federal mandate was issued.

If you need further proof of Silent Sound Spread Spectrum, a link to the US patent number 5159703 is included in the Resources section. The patent description specifies that it is for 'a silent communications system in which nonaural (cannot be heard) carriers in the ELF (Extremely Low Frequency) or VHF (Very High Frequency) range, or adjacent spectrums are frequency modulated with the desired intelligence (they are planted with the kind of emotion or thoughts they are designed to generate in people) and are propagated (sent out) acoustically (as sound) or vibrationally (as an energy frequency) for inducement into the brain (they are planted directly into the brain).

The patent compares this technology to audio books or CDs but that is far from the truth. It was scary enough for ex-President Eisenhower to issue a stern warning during his farewell address about the type, range, and scope of technology that was being used and developed for use against the citizens of the US and of the world.

The next time you are driving around, look for tall towers with round transmitters on all four sides. They may resemble cell towers but they are GWEN towers that transmit energy frequencies in the ELF, extremely low frequencies, and VHF, very high frequency, ranges, which are used in conjunction with HAARP to transmit energy into homes and businesses and are capable of implanting thoughts into the mind.

Have you noticed that all stores and restaurants now play background music, a new practice that I find bothersome and annoying. I have often wondered what is being broadcast in conjunction with the music and I found out a few years ago at a Barnes & Noble bookstore in Los Angeles. I was in the store with a friend and we both remarked that the music was very annoying. After fifteen minutes in the store I became so agitated, as did my friend that we put our selections down and walked out without buying anything. Whatever was being broadcast with the music was so distressing to me at an energetic level that I simply had to leave.

These towers emit frequencies that work with human energy control implants, specific chemical compounds, especially fluoride compounds, and the metallic elements contained in the chemtrails that are sprayed in the sky on a daily basis. Do you remember when the sky wasn't criss-crossed with white lines every day? I do and I notice the white lines now too. What are they spraying up there, and why hasn't the government done studies, issued reports, and addressed this issue? Maybe it's because the government is directly responsible for those white lines in the sky and it thinks we're too blind, stupid, or ignorant to notice them.

Evidence of this technology has become public in the past decade, although it has been the subject of continuous secret research for over seventy years. People are reporting a wide variety of side effects from it, ranging from headaches, fatigue, body aches, or illnesses that have no explanation. These reports are immediately discounted by the media as hypochondria, reported by mentally unstable people.

Consider the people who first reported having Morgellon's Disease in 2002 (which coincides with the occurrence of large numbers of chemtrails began appearing in the sky), a condition where fibers appeared under the skin, accompanied by a wide range of physical effects that include fatigue, health problems, skin rashes, and violent headaches. In spite of the ridicule and denial they received from the government and medical agencies, their physical symptoms were very real.

The medical community has stepped up to label anyone who reports having Morgellon's as mentally disturbed or delusional, but they can't deny the images of the fibers that can be seen under and protruding from their skin, as well as their debilitating and sometimes life threatening physical symptoms. No one has come forward to offer a solution, cure, or to admit that this is a form of implant designed to control human energy frequencies.

Strange physical reactions are one of the downsides of secret human energy controlling technology that can't be easily explained because people are experiencing symptoms from technology that isn't supposed to exist, resulting from experiments that are supposedly not being conducted. Since the programs are secret, illegal, and unethical, no one in the scientific community will admit that these experiments are being tested on the general public without their knowledge or consent. When the technology is unleashed on a large segment of the population a variety of side effects crop up as different people experience them in different ways, according to their natural energy frequency and level of vibration and awareness. Of course, it's all immediately denied by the media and the people who come forward are ridiculed and called schizophrenic and everyone is told that they are delusional, disturbed, and mentally unbalanced.

And yet what does happen to people who, like those who have Morgellon's disease, suddenly experience strange physical symptoms, who become ill and incapacitated, or who die, with no explanation? They are considered to be collateral damage in the ongoing attempts to control human energy.

Since the body has an electrical frequency at which it functions optimally, technology which disrupts that frequency can cause a wide range of physical and mental health issues. And this is a highly experimental work in progress, which means that the general population is the official test group and adjustments are made to the technology as people experience its effects.

We need to ask ourselves what other forms of technology are we unwittingly being subjected to and what side effects are they creating in us?

We know that vaccines are one delivery method for the energy control implants, is this why there is such a big effort to vaccinate people and especially children all over the world, despite the real dangers of serious health problems and death, and other side effects, that are overlooked, trivialized, or denied by governments, doctors, and the pharmaceutical community? And before you call me an anti-vaccine alarmist, remember that I was paralyzed by a vaccine, so I know this is real side effect because it happened to me. And today's vaccines contain far more toxic elements, including mercury, aluminum, and nano technology, than did the one that paralyzed me in 1963.

We are now learning that people like John Lennon's assassin were psychiatric patients and were involved in mind control programs. Have you noticed that all of the people involved in mass shootings in the past two decades have spent time in mental hospitals or been treated with some type of strong psychotropic drug? These are drugs that are designed to interfere with body chemistry in a way that affects energy flow and makes the recipient highly sensitive to mental, emotional, and energetic suggestion, including SSSS technology. It is possible that they have also been implanted with some kind of energy manipulation technology, along with being traumatized in mind control programs, that allows them to be controlled, in a very 'Manchurian Candidate' kind of way. They are no longer in control of themselves, their thinking, or what they do. This is what energy technology does, or is designed to do but it does not work that way on everyone and it doesn't always work the way it is intended to, which is a relief in the face of so much scientific and psychological terrorism.

While nanotechnology and implants have been introduced as the 'newest' form of medical devices in the past few years, they have been around for decades. In fact, we can trust that any technology shared with the general public has been in military or government use for at least two decades. Energy implants and the nanotechnology they utilize is not new technology and it is one way that your energy has been manipulated. Many of the energy control experiments conducted between the 1950s and

1970s used some form of implants which, together with memory erasing psychotropic drugs and traumatic abuse or torture, created the energy control programming that has tried, for over fifty years, to control the and manipulate the energy of the world's populations, with some degree of success.

Implants and energy technology are used to control energy in four ways:

Method #1: siphoning off energy where the implant or suggestion or frequency interference provides the host (you) with just enough energy to function and then feeds the rest to energy receivers, such as GWEN towers or HAARP,

Method #2: blocking energy where the implant or sugges-tion or frequency blocks the flow of energy within your body so you cannot access your higher energy frequencies, which includes your intuition, psychic abilities, compassion, and empathy,

Method #3: allowing energetic suggestion where the implant or suggestion or frequency is programmed to control your energy by manipulating your energetic frequency, and your thoughts, which is evident in people who are depressed, psy-chotic, schizophrenic, or who are called mentally ill or unsta-ble, and is also another way that GWEN towers and ELF transmissions are used, in conjunction with SSSS technology,

Method #4: inserting an energetic surrogate, or an energetic frequency that takes over your body and your energy, which causes consciousness blackouts or memory lapses. I call this energy hijacking and this may also involve the efforts of an 'energy assassin'.

Are you ready to learn about how these technologies work? Do you realize that many billions and possibly trillions of dollars have been poured into the development of these technologies? Every world government is active in these programs, and no matter what country or continent you live in or on, you can bet that your government is complicit in the use of this technology. From pervasive CCTV to internet spying to cell phone tapping to subliminal energy frequency transmissions that are used to control human thoughts and behavior, it is everywhere. But there are solutions and the first one is to understand what energy control technology is capable of and how it is used.

The Energy Siphons

Implants, frequencies, and devices that siphon energy work like someone using your unsecured wireless connection (which you may have thought was secured) without your knowledge. Although you don't know why your internet is working more slowly, it's because someone is connecting to it, using it, and slowing the speed of your connection. The siphoned energy is picked up by technologies that work in the same way a TV or radio picks up electronic signals, and they include the use of GWEN and HAARP technology, whose public patents specify that they transmit energetic frequencies for weather modification and human energy influence but they can both transmit and receive energetic frequencies of many different types, including human.

GWEN officially stands for Ground Weather Emergency Network, although its weather related use is secondary to its energy and mind control functionality. It should rightfully be called Global Wave Energy Network because that is what it is, a network of large towers, between 300 and 500 feet tall, placed around the U.S. 200 miles apart, with plans to extend them globally, to be used for global human energy control by the manipulation of brain waves or thought insertion.

These towers, which resemble cell towers, transmit at the VLF, Very Low Frequency, and ELF, Extremely Low Frequency, levels. The towers work in two stages, a network of copper wires fans out underground, at the base of the tower, transmitting energy through the ground, while the transmitters located high up on the towers transmit energy up to 300 miles away. Placing the towers 200 miles apart reduces the dead zones that occur at the outer edges of their 300 mile frequency range.

GWEN towers transmit energy at frequencies at levels designed to coordinate with intended mind control outcomes and that interfere with and manipulate the body's regular energetic frequencies. For example, to create depression, suicide, and general lack of motivation, an area can be inundated with energy at very or extremely low frequencies, using SSSS or Silent Sound Spread Spectrum technology that will create those feelings. Conversely, GWEN frequencies can be used to compel people to spend money, shop, or engage in specific activities. GWEN towers also work with HAARP technology.

HAARP stands for High Frequency Active Aural Research, another energy manipulating technology that sends energy beam pulses into the atmosphere, reflecting them off of the metals and substrates in chemtrails, to manipulate the jet stream and the atmospheric rivers which control the flow of water vapor around the world. HAARP technology emits highly concentrated, calibrated energy frequencies in the form of radio waves, sonic waves, or microwaves and it uses GWEN towers to transmit those frequencies to geographic areas. You need to understand HAARP and GWEN and how they work to know how energy siphons, implants, and other energy manipulating technology works.

When HAARP and GWEN are used to siphon energy, they send low energy frequencies into the atmosphere where they can be felt by the general population. This suggested energetic frequency is below the normal human resonance level. As people succumb to the energetic suggestion by 'feeling bad', the remaining balance of their energy is siphoned off and used to power future energetic transmissions. In this way energy control technology provides the initial blast of low frequency energy and then relies on the expected human response to that energy, to keep the energy cycling indefinitely.

It's like a feedback loop system, the initial blast of ELF energy triggers a response of depression or sadness, and if someone is experiencing those emotions and is at that energy level, they send their energy out in response to the ELF blast, which heightens and expands its reach and intensity, creating even more depression and sadness. The cycle continues until someone gets depressed and sad enough to commit suicide, hurt someone, or decides to raise their energy level and not feel depressed or sad.

Here's another example of how energy siphons work. Say the normal human energy frequency is 20, which can be sustained by conscious intention, and the manipulated energetic frequency level is 10, which is energy that humans are bombarded with, whose purpose is to lower the energetic frequency and siphon off the rest. The person feeling this low energy suddenly starts feeling sad, depressed, angry, and lowers their energetic frequency to the suggested level of 10 and the remaining balance of 10, which is part of their natural energy field, is now available for siphoning away by the GWEN towers. It's the equivalent of you having twenty apples in a basket and while you aren't looking I take ten of them away from you.

Low frequency energy impacts the body in different ways because it disrupts the body's natural energy rhythm and flow, the energy it needs to function optimally. Decreased energy flow can lead to mental depression, suicidal thoughts, lethargy, and feelings of helplessness and hopelessness. Your body needs all of its energetic resources to function optimally, and without access to its full energetic resources, it is at risk for a variety of compromising physical, mental, and emotional conditions.

As you can probably work out for yourself, these technologies seek out the lowest energy frequencies and use those to influence the general population. But this doesn't mean that if you have a high energy frequency you are immune to the energy siphoning form of human energy control technology. You may be a bigger target because your higher frequency is accompanied by a unique ability to expand your energy field. So if this technology can be used to lower your energy frequency, then the lower frequency energy siphoned from you has a greater reach and impact than that of others with a lower natural frequency.

Have you ever had a day when you felt strong mood swings, or you felt bad for no reason? That's how SSSS technology works, and how energy siphoning human energy control technologies are being used on you. And if you have been the victim of human energy or mind control experiments you may feel these energy swings more than other people because you have already been programmed to be a receiver for them.

Add to that the possibility of implants or other energy modulating devices in your body, and your body now becomes an energy receiver that can be influenced and manipulated by the energies which are being transmitted by GWEN towers and HAARP, as well as an energy transmitter, that is sending all kinds of energy to the GWEN and HAARP networks and related technologies whose purpose is to siphon off and manipulate your energy. I'll tell you how to deactivate this technology later in the book.

The Energy Blocks

Implants and human energy control technology that blocks energy flows works the same way that a governor works on an engine, which limits how fast the engine will allow the car to go, no matter how much you push the accelerator. If a governor is set at 55 mph, the car will never go faster than 55 mph. The energy control implants and associated technology that block energy flows limit the flow of energy to a specific frequency and output and no matter what you do, you cannot access any more energy even though you may be aware that more energy is available to you.

Have you ever wanted to do something and just could not get yourself to do it? Have you wanted to write a book, start a business, move to a new place, leave a relationship, or get a new job and even though you're unhappy or miserable and you want a change, you just cannot seem to make the change happen? This is what energy blocking technology does. It cannot block your thoughts but it can block the flow of energy so that the thought and action required to complete it do not connect with each other. It's like being in a car with no gas pedal, you can turn the car on but you cannot make it move.

Human energy blocking technology is one way that higher frequencies are modulated and lowered because the blocked energy leads to frustration, anger, resentment, fear, and other lower energies that can then be siphoned off and transmitted to GWEN towers or magnified with ELF energy technology. If your energy frequency is strong and high enough that blocking technology is used on you, then there is a recognition of your energetic uniqueness and a desire to use your energy for the control of others.

You can release the energy blocks, I explain how later in this book, but for a moment, give yourself an extra measure of appreciation for your special energy frequencies. I'm only partially joking here, because energy blocks are targeted to impact very high frequency people, to prevent them from expanding their energy fields to share their energy with others. By recognizing your own natural frequency, you make yourself a smaller target for this technology.

There is another reason for the use of energy blocking technology, especially in the generation born in the 1940s and 1950s, who became parents in the 1970s and 1980s. The generation of children they gave birth to is even more intuitive, sensitive, high energy, and empathic than they are, and the intention was to block the parents' energy so they could not give birth to children who were at a higher energy frequency, more intuitive, sensitive, and empathic than they were. But that didn't happen and in spite of the energy blocking technology and energy controlling implants, the generation of children born to these parents did fulfill their energy potential. So we have another very high energy generation on the planet that can continue the work of their parents.

Energy blocking technology can be removed by a simple process of realizing that it exists and then using your power and your energetic sovereignty to remove it.

The Energy Suggestors

Energy Suggestor implants and technology literally put thoughts in your head. They are pre-programmed with a range of emotions and energies that can be activated so you may decide to leave your family one day, or walk away from your home, or kill yourself or others, or start hearing voices and be declared mentally ill. This is a very destructive technology that has been used on people for decades, to control their behavior. Energy Suggestor implants and technology, based on the SSSS, Silent Sound Spread Spectrum, also work with GWEN, HAARP, and the ELF (Extremely Low Frequency) emissions, as well as powerful psychotropic drugs and post-trauma hypnotic suggestion, and have the broadest base of victims.

Thousands, perhaps millions, of people have been implanted with this kind of technology because it is the easiest to use in energy manipulation, within limits. The problem with this technology is that when it is used to control the energy of people who are naturally at a high energy frequency, it has unpredictable results because it is designed to work at low energy frequency levels.

The Energy Suggestor implants and technology were the most promising of the different types of energy control technologies because they were thought to be the most powerful and the easiest to implement on a mass level. It was believed that by broadcasting very low frequency energies or specifically programmed frequencies to crowds or masses of people that behavior could be controlled or created on demand.

So, a crowd could be induced to riot, as we saw in the 2015 riots in Ferguson, Missouri, or a large number of people in one area could be induced to commit suicide, undergo severe depression, or a large number of people would suddenly die, which was an intended purpose of this technology.

But the results that have been achieved are far different from the theories about how they should work. While some people can be induced to riot and create havoc, the Energy Suggestor implants and technology do not work on the people who were their ultimate target victims. In fact, as the overall population becomes more energetically aware, intuitive, sensitive, and more connected, cohesive, and congruent within their own energy fields, the general collective energy frequency rises and they have the opposite effect.

When the energetic frequency of the general population is high, the Energy Suggestor implants and the low frequency, destructive, and fear based energies being fed through them compel their intended victims to take action in an entirely different direction. They become more compassionate and empathetic with each other, and to initiate distrust and rebellion, rather than compliance and obedience, towards the 'official' presence.

The people this technology does work on is those who have a lower IQ, between 85 and 110, who have endured long-term and severe abuse and trauma, have been the victims of mind and energy control experiments, and those who are already mentally and emotionally unstable. It works best on people who are already highly energetically suggestible, which excludes the main target group, people at a high energy frequency.

And at this time, many people have tools to help them address, mitigate, and overcome their traumatic experiences. Something as simple as a desire to overcome trauma and to live with more joy is enough to overcome trauma's effects and release the effects of PTSD. De-sensitizing techniques, such as EMDR, Eye Movement De-Sensitization and Reprogramming, has been highly effective in brain reprogramming, even with veterans with extreme PTSD. Energy control technology has been planned for use in mass population control for decades, which is why there has been a big effort to put GWEN towers in place all around the world. But since the overall energetic frequency of the planet and of humanity is also rising, the entire project is failing because it is not designed to work with higher energy frequencies and has no effect on them. I believe that one of the flaws of this technology is the assumption that every human resonates at the same energy frequency, which is wrong. We all have different energy frequencies, according to our life history, emotional states, and energetic awareness. The more aware we are of ourselves as energetic beings, the greater our control over our own energy frequency, and the less susceptible we are to victimization, suggestion, and control by any kind of energy controlling technology.

The problem with Energy Suggestor energy control technology is that it is only effective within a specific range of lower energetic frequencies and it doesn't take into account the natural human desire for transcendence, connection, ascension, evolution, and congruence, the rise into higher frequencies that is the ultimate soul mission and the true purpose of life. Just as every parent strives to make life better for their children, every generation also strives to make the earth and the world a better place for future generations. Except, of course, those who want to control the world's people for their own power agendas.

Energy control technology is based on the principles behind Maslow's hierarchy of needs, which puts spiritual needs at the smallest top portion of a pyramid and life needs at the much larger bottom. Maslow's theory is wrong. Human energetic flow, movement, and expansion is spherical, not triangular. And spiritual needs are present at every level of the pyramid, not just at the top. Our desire to be spiritually aware and connected happens in conjunction with the achievement of all of our basic life needs, not after they are all met.

But it is hard to think about spiritual needs when you're hungry, homeless, and socially disenfranchised. It does explain why governments have expended great effort to ensure that populations experience lack, deprivation, financial depression, homelessness, and limited access to basic life comforts.

Have you noticed how there is some kind of economic or financial meltdown as a population begins to approach new levels of financial security, comfort, and prosperity? That happens because once people achieve stability in their living situations, they begin to reach new levels of spiritual awareness and are no longer afraid. And both mind and energy control technology function best when their victims are at a VLF (very low frequency) energy level so they are highly suggestible and can be controlled and manipulated.

Continuous wars and political maneuvering in the Middle East, Africa, and in Eastern Europe create mass refugee movements, as people flee guns, bombs, and death. But that is also a tool for energy control as fear not only drives people from their homes and disrupts their lives in a catastrophic way, these fearful people are then transplanted into less fearful areas, a current example is the influx of Syrian refugees into Western Europe. The media has already done its job of demonizing the refugees so the fear engine is primed and ready to go. The refugees have been stripped of every basic life support system so they are deeply afraid and their destined countries see them as a threat to their livelihoods and economies, so they are afraid too. And when fear meets fear, the result is another level of fear.

When basic life needs are the focus of one's existence, fear becomes the primary motivator, which keeps the human energetic frequency low and subject to energetic suggestion. And when those fears are augmented by additional threats to life, financial well being, or loved ones, the fear level rises exponentially. Add a million refugees, terrorist attacks which, staged or not, still inspire fear, and political, cultural, and religious bias and differences, and the fear energy portals are wide open.

When a population's life needs are easily met and people feel safe, secure, and are happy, their energetic frequency is high and it cannot be manipulated because it extends beyond the capabilities of Energy Suggestor human energy control technology.

That is why constant threats to peace, economic growth, and physical safety and security are so prevalent now. The world is not a more dangerous place, it is just made to appear more dangerous because when we're afraid we make ourselves available to energetic control and manipulation by Energy Suggestor technologies.

This is another energy control technology that can be de-activated so it is no longer effective.

The Energy Surrogate Technology

Energy Surrogate technology is a form of energetic hijacking, where one energetic presence is replaced with another. This is the form of energy control that utilizes ELF and more sophisticated brain altering technologies in the neurotronic and psychotronic weapons class. In its most basic form, Energy

Surrogate control technology takes over a body's energy field so that the person has the same physical presence but their energetic presence is totally different.

In the spiritual vernacular this is called a 'walk-in' but you won't find that word or term in the dictionary. A walk-in experience involves an energy displacing an existing energy in a physical body. This can be conscious or unconscious, voluntary or forced. In the case of Energy Surrogate technology, it is forced.

And if you have blanks in your memory, where you cannot remember parts of your life, as I shared with you in my own story of mind and energy control experimentation, or you are either acting in irrational or self destructive ways, or are incapable of taking action even though you may want to, you are most likely a victim of Energy Surrogate technology. A modern example is identity theft, where someone assumes another person's identity and then uses their credit and financial informa-tion to buy things that the actual owner would never buy.

With Energy Surrogate technology you can have the distinctive and very uncomfortable feeling that you are watching yourself from a distance, as an observer in your own life, like standing outside of your house looking in the windows at the strangers who have moved into and are now living in your home.

For Energy Surrogate human energy control technology to work in the best way, the incoming or surrogate energy and the host (you) must be at the same energetic frequency. Within a high energetic frequency range, an equivalent or higher energy can become an energy surrogate and the exchange is done on a voluntary level.

But with energy control protocols, the purpose behind using a surrogate energy is to use the host's energetic potential to expand pre-determined energy frequencies. The host (you) is used as a spokesperson, so to speak, for that energy because they have the ability to expand their energy field and they can embody large amounts of energy at a range of frequencies. This basic principle is heavily used in advertising, for example. If a well known person uses a product or service, it commands instant attention, everyone wants one.

By the same token, the energy levels that a high frequency person can embody makes them very attractive to other people, who want to connect to and be more like them. The energy that makes someone's appearance or voice or persona so charming is what makes than an attractive Energy Surrogate. But first, the Energy Surrogate has to be able to hijack the person's energy field and this is where the childhood energy and mind control testing created a back door for this eventual purpose.

Energy Surrogates are able to attach to an existing low energy trauma through a trauma marker in the energy field and replaces the host energy in a takeover or hijacking that is done without the host's approval or consent, and often without their knowledge.

The most effective setup for the effective and successful use of this type of energy control technology begins in childhood and represents the long term purpose of the use of child victims of human energy control programs and experiments. This is why many high energy, intuitive, empathic, and sensitive children were chosen for these programs because if traumatized enough, they could be come involuntary and highly accessible hosts for Energy Surrogate human energy control technology through the fear markers in their energy fields. This trauma-based fear becomes an unconscious portal or opening in their energy field, lowering their overall frequency and making them prime targets for future energy control technologies.

The purpose behind using high energy, intuitive, sensitive children, was to access bodies that were capable of holding high frequency energies and their expansive energy fields and replacing them, at some point in the future, with lower energy frequencies that could take advantage of the body's potential for energetic expansion but at much lower energy frequencies.

Let me go into this a little more because understanding the expansive nature of energy frequency is important in understanding the nature and purpose of Energy Surrogate human energy control technology. Lower frequency energy is very dense, is fear based, and it is limited to expanding in a linear fashion, it goes out in a straight line until it simply runs out of energy and stops. It also requires some type of outside input in order to stay viable, it is not self perpetuating. The only way to increase the amount and reach of lower frequency energy is to generate more of the fear that it needs to stay in motion.

Have you noticed how much more negative news reporting has become in the past fifteen to twenty years, how many staged terror events there are, such as false flag shootings and how intensely they are reported in the media? The daily bombardment of fear-provoking messages and information has one purpose, to create more fear so that the dense and lower frequency energy has a constant supply of energy that it requires to stay in existence, and it needs a very large and continuous supply to remain viable, especially with the current frequency rise and expansion that the human energy collective is undergoing now.

If we don't respond with fear, then the dense energy runs out of fuel and it stops. We have control over this process, we just need to remember that we do, and to use the power we have to choose our level and frequency of energetic vibration to stay in a fear-free zone.

Higher frequency energy is very light and expands exponentially, in a non-linear fashion. As it expands it goes outward in every direction, as an expanding sphere (think of blowing up a round balloon). Unlike fear-based, dense energy higher frequency energy is self generating, it is its own source and supply, as long as it is fueled with the smallest amount of positive intention. The tiniest desire for peace, joy, love, prosperity, or well being is enough to start expanding higher frequency energy. And just as light always overtakes darkness, dense energy will always give way to higher frequency, higher vibration energy. That's why it is so important to express gratitude, to set intentions for our most powerful, brightest outcomes, to expand what we feel happy about, because it doesn't take much high vibration, high frequency energy to expand and overcome fear and dense energy.

The physical bodies that can hold dense energy (think of people like psychopaths and mass murderers) do not have the ability to hold higher frequencies and cannot expand their energy exponentially the way people who have higher frequencies can. But, if a dense, fear-based energy is placed in a body that can hold a high frequency energy field, then the dense energy can be expanded exponentially like the higher frequency energy. That's the hypothesis that Energy Surrogate human energy control programming assumes, but the reality is much different.

When the expanded dense energy encounters the body's natural desire for a higher frequency state, there is a conflict and the person can either have a psychotic break or reject the energy entirely. This type of energy control technology is used in the MKUltra Monarch program, whose victims include many of today's top celebrities. In fact, they must be willing to cross that threshold if they are to enjoy the level of success which is oddly only available to a select few. They pay a heavy price for their success as they must agree to allow their energy to be completely controlled since they are nothing more than a tool to control mass behavior, opinion, and emotions.

Many of them have had psychotic breaks in the past few years, exhibiting strange behavior like shaving their head, having very public breakdowns, excessive drug and alcohol use, acting out in inappropriate, sexually suggestive ways, or losing control of themselves and of their lives.

These psychotic breaks occur due to the conflict between the dense energy programming they are subjected to and their energy field's inability to handle large amounts of dense, negative energy. If the body's energy frequency is high enough and the person has even a small amount of awareness of their energy and knows how to control it, then the Energy Surrogate technology is rejected.

No matter how much the Energy Surrogate control programmers want to flood a body with dense, negative, dark energy to expand it in the same way that lighter, higher energetic frequencies expand, the natural human energetic frequency core state is kindness, compassion, love, and divinity. Depending on the strength of the core energy and the host's overall frequency, Energy Surrogate human energy control technology's effects can result in a total takeover or a mild annoyance, like the difference between a full blown case of the flu or a mild cold.

When we intentionally focus on our energetic state and keep our energy high, Energy Surrogate human energy control technology is completely ineffective, although it is the most powerful tool in the human energy control programming arsenal.

One way to understand why this technology fails in high energy level people is to look at the energy control delivery system, which is called ELF, for Extremely Low Frequency. It works in an extremely low frequency range and if one's energy frequency is high, low frequencies are ignored or rejected. We all react to ELF frequencies in different ways. In my bookstore experience, for example, I had to leave the store because it made me feel very agitated and I knew that something was happening. If you hear certain types of music, like heavy metal or violent rap, do you turn up the volume or turn the radio off? That's how you would react to ELF transmissions.

In order for this technology to work effectively and have the desired mass impact, it would have to deliver much higher energy frequencies but then those would connect with the host energy field's higher frequencies and that would expand the higher frequency energy and make people feel better, not worse. It would make them more loving, compassionate, kind, positive, benevolent and ultimately, not controllable, psychotic, or psychopathic. At worst, ELF waves would cause mild feelings of fatigue, depression, anxiety, a desire to sleep, and a lack of motivation.

As the overall energetic frequency and vibration of the planet increases, the ability of a human body to hold dense energy decreases proportionally. So as we collectively raise our vibes, the dense energy frequencies have fewer places or bodies to occupy and who are willing to hold this energy. And this further decreases the ability of any type of human energy controlling technology to work.

You need to understand this to understand how Energy Surrogate technology works because it is activated by the trauma markers created by severe trauma and its ensuing compartmentalization, detachment, and emotional disconnection, a major component of all mind and energy control technology. In order for the energy surrogate or walk-in energy to have access to a body's energy field, there must be a corresponding dense energy frequency marker available for it to access.

These are the energetic markers created during trauma programming that the walk-in or surrogate energy can use, at any time, to gain access to the energy field. Severe traumas, as mentioned earlier, include rape, torture, deprivation, electric shock, drugs, shame, humiliation, isolation, rejection, and fear. This is why MKUltra and other mind and energy control programs use trauma as their primary tool for control, it gives them a powerful access point into their victims' energy field that they can use at any time, for any purpose because while the victim doesn't have any conscious memory of what happened to them, their mind and energy field do.

When a victim is traumatized over the long term, their mind compartmentalizes the trauma and stops remembering it on a conscious level, but it remains in the subconscious mind and in the energy field. The trauma contains a very high level of fear and this is the energetic marker or access point that a surrogate energy needs to attach to and walk into the energy field.

If the trauma occurs at a young age, when the energy field is very strong and clear, the trauma markers are much stronger because infants and young children have an unfiltered expectation of kindness, love, compassion, and care. When they are traumatized, brutalized, and treated with sadistic, indifferent cruelty, and that experience is repeated over days, weeks, months and even years, the shock is immediate, powerful, and is imprinted in their developing energy system.

Very young children develop neural pathways in response to their environment and any trauma is added to those neural pathways so it becomes an expected part of their environment and they develop a trauma response that overrides any other response, including compassion. Children who have this type of trauma response permanently embedded in their neural pathways are diagnosed with 'attachment disorder', and are considered to be untreatable by conventional psychological and psychiatric methods. They are capable of violent rages, cruelty, are devoid of compassion, and are considered highly dangerous to those around them. They are the children who murder their families or set fire to a home.

While they become consciously unaware of the trauma due to the mind's ability to compartmentalize and 'forget' painful memories, the energy field holds that trauma and traumatic memory in place. The energy field then becomes easily accessible through triggers and key words that awaken the trauma on an energetic level and allow the Energy Surrogate technology to take over. It is a horrible testament to the lengths that these people will go to control human energy.

If your energy or mind control experimentation included trauma, then you probably received psychotropic drugs, powerful pharmaceuticals that erased memories so you couldn't consciously remember what happened to you. These drugs work in the same way that surgical anesthesia works. While they are in effect, your body still functions but you have no memory of what has happened or what was done to you. If you have ever had surgery, you know that when you wake up the surgery has happened but you don't remember any of it. The drugs mask the conscious memory but they do not hide the unconscious memory, or the disruption to the energy field that was caused by the trauma. And that is what the Energy Surrogate energy control technology is designed to take advantage of.

When the Energy Surrogate takes over, there is a disconnect with one's awareness that can range from total black-outs of days, weeks, months, or years of your life, to what feels like short term memory loss. When the Energy Surrogate implant is successful, the behavior then becomes distinctly different. You may find yourself doing and saying things that are out of character for you and they are, because you have been hijacked on an energetic level and you are no longer in control of your body, your mind, or of your energy field. This is something that I have experienced and I can remember, especially in my twenties, feeling like I was being controlled by strings, like a puppet, as I watched myself doing things that I did not want to do but that I could not stop doing.

Depending on the level of trauma, the person's basic energetic frequency, and the type of energy technology used, it is possible for a person to drastically change their behavior and commit murder, rob a bank, or engage in extremely destructive acts. Notice how every person who has been accused of some type of mass shooting or crime has spent time in mental institutions, many have been in military service, and have been treated with strong psychotropic drugs for 'mental illness'.

For most people, though, Energy Surrogate technology involves behavior that is more self destructive or self limiting, in ways that slow their progress or interfere with their life or their dreams. Remember that these technologies were designed to harness or limit the energy of people who would be a force for positive change in the world, so they will block or limit their ability to take action on their purpose, goals, and objectives in any way they can.

Sometimes the surrogate arrives in the form of a distracting, destructive, or manipulative person, I call these people 'energy assassins'. This can be a family member, a romantic connection or a close friendship and can manifest as a strong attraction or a strong need to help someone you feel 'needs' you in some way. The trauma that is part of the energy and mind control conditioning hijacks a high energy person's empathic abilities so they become attracted to people who are wounded or damaged in some way and believe that it is their life purpose to heal or fix them, they are meant to be together, and they will do all they can to ensure that the relationship works, no matter how destructive or abusive it is. That person has been placed in your life to connect with the trauma markers and interfere with your energy in some way.

Energy assassins are intentionally and deliberate placed in your life to derail or sidetrack you. For example, if you have big plans for your life and you get into a serious accident or you meet someone who engages with you in a way that disrupts your life, or you abandon your plans to be with them, that person could be an energy assassin. These people won't kill you, in the modern assassin context, but they are capable of disrupting your energy field and eventually connecting to you as an Energy Surrogate. Have you ever been involved in a romantic relationship that took over your life? That's an energy assassin at work.

Or you may experience what you call a failure early in your life and it prevents you from believing that you are capable of success. Think of the people and situations that suddenly appear in your life and you connect with them in a way that disrupts your life. Have you ever done that and asked yourself what you were doing, as you were moving into that situation?

This is Energy Surrogate technology at work through an energy assassin. Your energy gets hijacked and while you may, on some level, be aware that you do not want to do whatever you are doing, you feel powerless to stop yourself. The results can be emotionally, physically, and mentally devastating, and that is their purpose.

You may also experience emotions that are out of character for you, like extreme anger, shame, guilt, or fear. The Energy Surrogate energy control connects through the access points that were created by the trauma you experienced and while you may not remember it, it is still very much part of your memory and your energy field. I now know that my energy control trauma included shame and humiliation because throughout my life they have been strong trigger points for me, as well as being the situations where my energy flow gets stuck.

To know what your trauma was, think about what you try to avoid, what triggers you, what makes you feel terrible, and what you react most strongly to. Consider the kind of people and situations that distract you, that you feel sorry for, that you feel you need to help. These are the most likely candidates for your 'energy assassins'. But, like all other energy control technologies, Energy Surrogate human energy control systems can be deactivated and all trauma markers and access points deactivated and/or removed. We'll cover that in the next section.

.

THE ANTI-ENERGY CONTROL
SOLUTIONS

If you're angry and upset after reading about this energy control technology, and you want to get revenge or take action, you're not alone. When I realized that this had happened to me and I finally started putting the pieces of my life together, filling in the blanks with the knowledge I could gather from others' experiences, I had a range of emotions from anger to disbelief to confusion. I was angry that it had happened, angry that my parents had allowed me to be the victim of energy control experimentation, whether it was intentional or unintentional, couldn't believe that this type of activity was taking place on such a large scale, and confused as to why it had happened to me.

I was a child when I was involved in the mind and energy control testing but, in the eyes of those who want to wield unlimited power and control over the world's populations so they can tell everybody what to do, amass all of the money, and to rule everything, I was a powerful means to a potentially powerful end. Learning to control the highly intuitive, sensitive, high frequency energy that I had, as did many children of my generation, was a very powerful tool that could be used to control the world, its people, and all of its energy. It had the potential to be such a powerful tool that governments, actual and shadow, along with their alien counterparts and masters, were willing to do anything to learn how to control it. Which is what they did and they are still doing it today.

You may have felt a range of emotions as you were reading this information and started putting the missing pieces of your life together. That is the early phase and it is challenging but you can move through it and access the levels of release and closure you need to rid yourself of this energy controlling programming.

There is nothing about this technology, its purpose, and how it is being used, that is right or beneficial, ethical, or valuable, but it has happened and I know that it is still happening. It could be used for good, but it isn't being used that way. We are not powerless in the face of these awful experiments and programs, although you may be feeling that way right now. We can do something about them because the one thing that energy control programs, technology, implants, surrogates, and experiments cannot do is work on higher frequency energy. They are absolutely powerless beyond a fairly low frequency. So all we have to do is keep our energy high and we will be beyond their control.

But what do you do if you know that you have been the victim of energy and mind control and maybe have an implant or walk-in, have an energetic marker or access point, and have experienced the trauma that has already impacted your life? You can take care of that too, and I'll show you how.

The first thing you will want to do is let yourself be angry about this because you need to express your anger and get it out of your system. Anger you hold in becomes another marker that makes you a target for Energy Surrogates and it lowers your energy frequency, which also makes you a prime target for other human energy controlling technology.

Just remember that if you were born in the 1940s to the early 1980s, your parents were conditioned to obey authority without question, they did what they were told to do, and they believed that the government was doing things that were in their best interests. It would not have occurred to them to question the government's request to take their children away or to conduct tests on them.

And they were probably lied to about whatever was actually being done. Or they were told that a career or reputation rested on their complicity and agreement. In those days, reputation was everything and people would do anything to protect their reputations, even volunteering their children for 'research'.

Most parents would not willingly allow their child to be drugged, tortured, abused, and implanted but if they didn't know what was being done and the child's memory was erased, they had no way of knowing what was happening.

If you want to be angry, be angry with the governments and secret organizations that engage in this activity, and everyone who is complicit, especially the military, scientific, psychiatry, and psychology communities who provide the research facilities, drugs, technology, and methodologies to conduct these experiments. And then put your anger to good use so you not only end the effects of this mind control experimentation on yourself, you also help end it for everyone else.

As I said earlier, human energy control technology and implants only work with very low frequency energy. They have a much less significant effect on higher frequencies. And in fact, once you begin to remember your life, to put the pieces together, to understand what happened to you and start regaining control over your life, the implants and any other technology stops being effective, it simply stops working. Why? Because it needs your energetic agreement, fear , anger, and lower frequency energy to work. If you do not agree to be influenced by this energy, consciously or unconsciously, it will not work on you. For example, what happens if you put anything but gasoline in your car's gas tank, like sugar or salt or sand? The engine will be ruined and it won't work (it's true, please do not try this at home on your car). It still looks like a car and has all of its parts, but a significant component of it has been deactivated (the engine) and it won't work.

All energy control technology works with fear-based energy systems and cannot function with higher energy because its purpose is to block our access to and use of higher frequency energy. So by raising our energy frequency, we block the human energy controlling technology and render it ineffective.

How do you raise your energy? It's a matter of belief and intention. If you have read any of my work, you know that I am an Energy Savante™, and an expert on energy transformation, intention, alignment, and manifestation. I know that we are, at our core, a collection of energetic frequencies that we access through our beliefs and intention. In every moment we are using energy, via the power of our thoughts, to create our individual and collective realities. We can have a more positive impact on the outer reality, our lives and the world, through the force of our intention, from our beliefs and thoughts, when we don't allow any limited results we see in our reality become the set point for our intention.

In other words, the universal Law of Cause and Effect applies here -- we are the cause of everything in our reality and what we see and experience is an effect, result, or outcome. If we want to change the effect (result) we have to change the cause, or change what we are doing. If I want to stop being unhappy, for example, I have to stop being sad because my being sad is the cause of the effect or outcome of unhappiness that is in my reality.

It is a very simple process that only appears to be complicated. Each one of us has the ability to move energy any way we want to. If you have ever wanted something to happen and it did, or you created a 'miracle' and manifested something you really wanted, that's how energy works. With a strong intention, accompanied by an equally powerful desire and belief, you can create miracles that move mountains. You have the power to do this, believing it is the first step.

One way to start the process of transformation and energy movement is to look at it as an energy exchange, trading out one energy for another by looking at what you want to feel instead of what's currently going on within you. If you're feeling sad and want to be happy, you must be willing to stop being sad and find a more fulfilling emotion to replace it.

You also have to remember that we are energetic beings, we have an energy field and are part of a universal energy field, we interact with each other and with the world through energy. This is also the knowledge that was first spearheaded by Tesla over a century ago, which gave birth to the human energy control protocols. If you keep that in mind, you can see that all of reality is simply a huge flow of energy that creates according to whatever we think, believe, and intend.

If you want to make a cake, you must start with the right ingredients. You can't have cake if you use ingredients to make a meatloaf. So in this case your 'cake' is what you decide you want in your life. Giving any energy to fear or to fear-based thinking, and that includes anger towards those who have hurt you or who have tried to manipulate you through manipulative energy technologies, starts replacing your cake ingredients with those needed for meatloaf, and this makes your energy field controllable.

Their motives were not kind, just, or pure, but they win if you allow them to continue to manipulate you through fear or anger at what has happened to you. And your anger, no matter

123

how justified it is, allows the energy control technology to remain in charge of your energy.

> You are sovereign in your life and you have control over your life and everything that happens in it.
> You are sovereign over your energy and you have control over everything that is in your energy field.

Even if you have been subjected to the worst of the mind and/or energy control experiments, you have energy implants, or you have been subjected to psychotropic drug therapy, or you have an Energy Surrogate or walk-in, you are still in control of your life and energetic realities, when you take intentional control over them. Once you claim your authority and sovereignty, no outside interfering energies can have any impact on you.

And you claim your authority by setting intentions for your life, include declarations that you want to be rich, happy, and successful, you want to be in joy and enjoy your life, you want to have loving, respectful, kind, supportive, and honorable people in your life, and you want to live your life in a powerful, fulfilling way. This has to become a daily practice for each of us; at this time we cannot afford to do otherwise.

124

We are surrounded by energy technology that is bombarding us with low frequency energy every minute of the day. These energy waves are designed to amplify the lowest energy frequencies and make you feel bad, unhappy, afraid, confused, hopeless, depressed, and powerless. And they target those energies to amplify them and supply fuel to the ongoing dense energy containers. If you're holding any of those low frequency energies in your own energy field, you are a prime target for manipulation and control by these human energy control technologies.

The only solution is to 'raise your vibes', to maintain your energetic frequency at the level you want it to be, and to keep your energy field clear of any fear and other elements that lower your energy frequency.

As you read about the four different kinds of energy control technologies, did any of them feel familiar to you? Did you make any connections between them and what you believe has happened to you? Removing or de-activating those implants is a simple matter of commanding that they be de-activated, as you raise your energy frequency. They work with energy, so if you shift your energy to a level they cannot work with, they will no longer work in the way they are supposed to.

To put this in a simpler context, imagine a lamp with a blue light bulb in it. The blue light is hard to read and see by, and you don't like it but you put up with it because you don't know how to change it. One day you decide to replace the blue light bulb with a white one and you are determined to figure out how to do that. You get the bulb changed and now you can see and read clearly.

Why didn't you do that sooner? Because we make changes when we are ready for them and the desire to change and the action required to change usually happen on different levels. You may want to make changes but until you're ready to take action, you'll continue to be frustrated and annoyed, but not do anything about the situation. The moment your pain and annoyance threshold is reached, you'll change the light bulb.

When you are tired of feeling powerless and unhappy, when you want to change your life and you're ready for the changes to happen, that's when you make changes, and not one minute sooner. I have written that "We change when the pain of staying where we are becomes greater than our fear of change." And then when you do make changes, let the change become a new beginning. Don't judge yourself for anything you did in the past. That just creates fear and more trauma, which is what you want to get away from.

126

If you are ready to learn about the energy technology removal, disengagement, and de-activation processes, here they are by technology type:

Energy Siphons Release

Energy siphons work by siphoning off your energy, like a bypass hose that is attached to your energy field. To know what is being siphoned off, think about what you do not have the energy, motivation, or courage to do.

Where in your life do you feel you have no energy?

What are your strongest emotions and where do you feel out of control, frustrated, and angry?

Do you have any unfinished life business to complete?

Are you waiting for something to happen to take action?

What happens if you take action right now?

What do you wish you were doing instead of what you are doing right now?

Is there any place in your life where you feel disempowered? Can you start taking steps to change that situation?

Practice breathing exercises to help you ground and center your energy. Set aside a few minutes each day to breathe deeply in and out, consciously being aware of your lungs filling up and releasing the air, count your breaths, start with five at first and focus all of your awareness on breathing. This will help you re-center your energy and make you aware of your energy field's boundaries.

Imagine gathering your energy together and bringing it all into your body. How does it feel when you are surrounded by your own power?

What does having strong energy boundaries look and feel like to you? If you had strong energy boundaries that allowed you to feel more in control of your life and what was in it, what would not be in your life right now? What would be in your life instead? What do you want to have in your life right now?

Bringing your energy together to focus on what you want in your life creates a container of intention for that energy to flow into, and it moves you out of regret and sadness into a more positive, action oriented way of thinking. If you want to stop the energy siphons, you have to remove the things that are siphoning your energy and that begins with your thoughts and what you spend your time thinking about.

Stay focused in the present moment and for a few minutes, close your eyes and notice your breath as you breathe in and out a few times. Listen to the sounds of the world around you, especially the sounds of nature. This helps connect you to the earth and to your home, and will help re-center and re-ground your energy in higher frequencies.

How do you know what the present moment is? It is the moment in which you are breathing because it's the only moment you have. Breath is our dual connection to the spiritual and material world, it's also absolutely essential to life, and is something we do every minute of the day and night. Each moment in which you are breathing is the present moment, that's why focusing on breath and breathing is an effective grounding and centering tool.

As you start thinking of what is not happening in your life, what you do not have the time and energy to do, write them down as positive affirmations and intentions, using words like "I am", "I will" and other positive words that will help expand these things in your life. This will both raise your frequency because you're no longer blaming or shaming yourself for what you are not doing, and it will also remove the human energy control technology that is siphoning off your energy. And it ensures that you have full use of your energy because your frequency is higher and you have a conscious, determined, intentional focus for your energy.

The only way energy siphons can work is if you aren't paying attention to where your energy is going or what you are focusing on, and allow your energy to be scattered by the distractions of self   judgment, criticism, blame, shame, guilt, doubt, and fear.

Energy Blocks Release

Energy blocks work by blocking your access to your energy. You feel stuck, like you're spinning in circles, or like a car that is in neutral gear -- no matter how hard you press on the gas pedal, the car won't go anywhere.

To remove the blocks you have to bring your goals and dreams back into focus.

What do you want to do with your life that you aren't doing today?

What dreams have you put away that can now be brought forward?

Focusing on a goal allows you to access more of your energy because you are focused on what you want to do, rather than what you cannot do or have not done.

Setting positive intentions for what you want creates pathways for energy to flow into. Our human form is an energy container and we use it to receive energy and manifest it into the form we call our reality. An intention creates a template for energy to download into, like pouring water into a glass. Strong intentions, together with positive, empowered, focused beliefs, create bigger energy containers.

Despite the fact that we see ourselves as 'mere' human beings, we are actually much more than that on an energetic level. We create the reality we live in individually and collectively, and our positive, high vibe individual efforts contribute to the energetic and frequency expansion of our collective reality. This is a mission we must each rise to if we want to avoid the disastrous outcome of living in a world where our will is subservient to energy control technology.

And as you set bigger goals, you begin to gather more of your energy to your goals, and that releases the energy blocks in an organic way. This isn't something you can force and if you do that you just start judging and criticizing yourself, which begins the cycle of self blaming or shaming and makes you more suggestible and susceptible to energy blocking technology.

Pay attention to who you blame for your limitations, lack of success, life results, and experiences. Anger and regret are empowering only when they are used to create more anger and regret; they are disempowering in every other way. They represent a choice as to how you are going to use your energy and are disempowering when you want to feel anything else. We can use anger to respond in hindsight to an injustice, betrayal, abuse, or a judgment, in a limited and ineffective way because all of things are in the past, and we cannot do anything to change them.

Or we can rise beyond our anger, no matter how justifiable it is, and stay in the present moment where only the potential future exists, and set intentions for what we want now, because now is all that matters. The past has no power unless we invite it to become part of our present reality.

So start with a small goal you know you can accomplish, write out your steps and take action on something every day. Break your actions down into small steps if you have to, just try to do something every day. Be sure to celebrate every single victory too, as this re-aligns you with your energy and allows your energy field to expand into higher frequencies.

Energy Suggestion Release

Energy Suggestion technology is a form of mind control that uses your own energy to manipulate you. Because it is like having words put in your mouth, as you learned about the Silent Sound Spread Spectrum technology, releasing this form of energy control involves a change in thinking and behavior.

What are you doing that you do not want to do?

What are you feeling that you do not want to feel?

What kind of negative, self defeating thoughts are you thinking right now that are creating those things in your reality and you no longer want to think them?

How many negative things do you say about yourself, things like "I am not lucky", "nothing good ever happens to me," or "I will never....," "I can't ..."

Those words are an open invitation to Energy Suggestion human energy control technology to attach itself to your lower, negative, dense energy and amplify it.

It is your natural state to be rich, happy, and successful, how far away from that state are you? What does it take to get you to that state – remember that every creation begins with an intention. The moment you decide you want something else or you deserve something better is the best time to begin to make changes. This is what I refer to in my Energy Congruence Coaching programs as your 'point of power', the moment where you are at your most powerful crossroads where you can energetically multi-task to create change. You can acknowledge that you are not satisfied with your life, you are ready to consider other options, and are ready to make a decision. This is a critical moment that can be used to either push you back into an angry past or into a more joyful future. To avoid overwhelming yourself, it is best to avoid judging yourself for anything you have done prior to that moment, to focus on one thing at a time and to make changes slowly.

Each day, and as often as you can remember to, focus on what being happy means to you and work backwards from the outcome. For example, if you want to be happy and that is your outcome, what does that mean to you? What does your life look like when you're happy? Do you live somewhere else, have a different job or are self employed? Are you single or in a relationship? Start filling in those details and 'happy' becomes more personal and achievable.

Use writing, journaling, and question and answer to help you identify those things that are important and meaningful to your happiness.

Be honest and reasonable too. You may want to win the lottery or have a million dollars and that's a great long term goal but money is not the issue, what you think that money will buy, the kind of life you can have, the problems you will no longer have, the freedom you will have with that money, that's what having money means to you.

Use those meanings as the focus point for what will make you happy. Then direct your attention and energy to what can you do today to make yourself happy right now. Don't just focus on the big things; focus on the little things too. Keep your focus on the present because the future is created from what we do in each present moment.

Do one thing that makes you happy each day, nothing is too small or insignificant, so don't judge anything you do. For example, if it makes you happy to watch the sun rise, then do that as often as you can. If it makes you happy to spend ten minutes enjoying a cup of tea, do that every day. You may feel uncomfortable or strange doing this at first, so take very small steps and celebrate every victory and every bit of progress that you make.

And remember that each thought and belief has energy, so pay attention to your thoughts every day. As a particular thought or belief comes to mind, ask yourself whether you want to energize it.

Are you willing to live with the outcomes it is going to create?

Is it a thought that is going to add to the misuse of your energy and extend an invitation to energy control?

Do you want to see the results of that thought in your own life and in the world now?

Once you have identified those thoughts, change them to reflect a different level of energy. All thoughts have equal creative power, keep that in mind as you decide how you are going to use the power and energy of your thoughts to create your reality.

As you re-integrate into your own energy you will find it easier to do things that make you happy, that bring you joy, and it will become more natural. But as you have not had access to this aspect of yourself for a long time, or there are traumas associated with the mind control conditioning, it may feel strange or uncomfortable at first. Since this type of energy control technology is found in people who are depressed or mentally unstable, be sure to get the counseling you need too, if you feel that will help you, as that will help in your recovery.

Energy Surrogate Release

The Energy Surrogate technology has the most dramatic effect, in the short and longer term, as it hijacks your energy field using existing trauma markers as entry points. It may have been far more effective when you were younger than it is today, so you may not be as susceptible to it today as you may have been in the past. But you may have done things in the past that you regret, even if you feel you had little or no control over yourself or your actions.

One of the ways to de-activate this technology is to stop regretting the past and to give yourself closure with anything you have done that you now regret. 'You can't unring the bell' as the saying goes, and you cannot undo anything that was done in the past. But you can make the present a new, brighter, happier, and more powerful experience.

If you know you have experienced trauma, get help to get over it, if that's what you need.

If you feel you are strong enough mentally, emotionally, spiritually, and psychically to do it yourself, make it part of your daily practice to focus your intention on keeping your energy field clear, high, intact, and bright by releasing all energy scattering or distracting elements out of it, which are things like judgments, criticisms, negative thoughts and beliefs, emotions, and fear.

You do not have the luxury of anger or fear because those represent the Energy Surrogate's access points. So you have to choose -- you can be angry about what was done to you or you can stop the process right now and close off all access points so you can start being in full control of your own energy field again. Forgiveness is essential, as is disconnection from the past and acceptance of everything that has happened in your life until now.

A quick word about forgiveness and what it actually means because it is highly misunderstood and misinterpreted. It is a way to energetically disconnect from energies you no longer want to be connected to. That's why some say that it's the gift you give to yourself, it is a way of unburdening yourself from carrying energy around that you do not want to carry. It is not a blanket absolution or pardon to everyone who has ever been mean or unkind to you.

Forgiveness has nothing to do with the other person or situation, it is all about you. You forgive to let go of or release energy. Or, in other words, your forgiveness gives the person who hurt you the gift of their own energy. If you see it that way, what you can include in your forgiveness is easy to do and it feels better than thinking you have to be nice to everyone who has ever been mean to you and pretend like nothing ever happened between you. That is not what forgiveness is about at all. It is nothing more than a process through which you release yourself from the burden of energy you no longer wish to carry. So make a list and start re-gifting that energy that you no longer want to be part of your energy field.

This is the one energy control technology that requires conscious intention to keep it turned off and to make you unavailable, so affirming your control over your own energetic sovereignty, mastery, and control is vital. Using powerful affirmations in moments where you feel weak, unsupported, or afraid is important to your progress. Having strong energy boundaries is critical to your healing from this type of manipulation, and that doesn't mean keeping everyone out of your life.

Energy boundaries are how we define the energy in our life, and my favorite energy boundary that I have shared with millions of clients, students, and audiences is

"Everyone in my life loves, honors, and respects me and everything in my life is a source of love, peace, and joy."

You can use that one or create your own. It works but you have to use it often. The important thing with this type of human energy control technology is to maintain a conscious awareness of your energy, what you are empowering, and what is happening in your life.

You also need to pay attention to the people in your life, who you are attracted to and who wants to connect with you. Be very clear about what kind of relationships you want to have, by using strong energy boundaries, and that will prevent any energy surrogates from attaching themselves to your energy field. If you think this is weird, remember that all of our connections to people start with an energy connection. When a connection doesn't feel good or feel right, or when it conflicts with your energy boundaries it represents a threat that you should avoid.

Also avoid the temptation to feel sorry for people, or to align yourself with people who need you or who try to take advantage of you in some way. Your response to them is your way of knowing how you are trying to heal your trauma and pain through others. We cannot heal ourselves by healing others, but we can be an example of healed and whole energetically congruent living by first attending to our own healing.

Recovering from any kind of energy control technology is a process and there is no quick fix. Expect to go through a grief process first, as you mourn your wounds and feel that you have been wronged. This is normal and you have been wronged in a very dishonest, unethical, mean, thoughtless, inconsiderate, disrespectful, and harmful way. But every wound eventually heals if we give ourselves the time, space, and loving mindfulness that allows it to heal.

Then you get to the 'fun' part, deciding how you are going to use your energy and what you want to create. It is the nature of energy to flow and to create, so you are using energy in the best way when you use it to create new realities for yourself.

Take it day by day and do something that grounds your energy in powerful, positive intentions for your life every day.

THE STATE OF ENERGETIC
CONGRUENCE™

In spite of all of the dire consequences that can arise out of the human energy control protocols, we have many options to create different and more positive outcomes, as long as we remember that it's the power, magnificence, and creative aspects of our energy that the human energy control establishment wants. As I have said before, they need us far more than we need them and if they really wanted to get rid of us, they have the weapons, tools, and ability to do that many times over.

But there is a reason they don't and it's that they need us and they need to be able to use and control our energy for whatever control and domination agendas they have. So rather than being the losers in this game, we have the upper hand, as well as the potential to win in a very big way, if we learn to use, focus, and control our energy in ways that serve us individually and collectively. And the best way to do that is to understand and apply the concept of 'Energetic Congruence™".

Energy flows like water and it will go in any direction and follow any path until it encounters something that blocks it.

Then it will either flow around the block, if it can, or start building up behind the block until it eventually flows over it. But the water doesn't stop flowing (unless we turn it off), and neither does energy.

Energy is also non-judgmental and will morph into anything we create. Every thought and belief is equally powerful – energy doesn't judge our thoughts or beliefs, refusing to go in a certain direction because it isn't fulfilling or aligned with our outcomes. The thought that "I'm never going to be happy" is just as powerful and receives just as much energy as the thought "I am blissfully happy now and always." In fact, the thought that has the greatest emotional intensity and fear is going to get more energy, because it is usually the one you have most of your belief system invested in.

And energy flows to all of our thoughts and beliefs, powering all of them. While we don't have a limited supply of energy, we do not function well when we are trying to energetically multi-task, especially if those many tasks are not aligned or congruent, meaning they do not have the same focus, level of frequency, and are not going in the same direction.

If you want to be happy but you're doing a lot of things that are not making you happy, then your energy flows are moving in different directions, they are not congruent, working in harmony, aligned with a strong intention, you're trying to focus on being happy while a lot of your energy is distracted by unhappiness or a similar energy.

In order to be happy you will have to give up a lot of what is not making you happy. And until you do, you will be happy sometimes and unhappy the rest of the time. When you're unhappy you will be thinking about the next time you can be happy, and when you're happy, you will be wondering how long it's going to last until you are unhappy again.

Do you see how this channels your energy into many different directions, very few of them going towards what you really want, which is to be happy? Your energy is conflicted and many people live their lives this way, following one life path and wishing they were doing something else. This is called being energetically uncongruent. And it makes us highly susceptible to energy and mind control technologies because they connect to fear, doubt, insecurity, and anxiety, which all reflect and represent various types of energy trauma.

The key to being whole and fulfilled, and impervious to any kind of energetic manipulation, is to have all of our energy flowing in the same direction, working in harmony, with deliberate and conscious focus, and which brings us ever closer to being congruent. We do that by forming strong intentions, which

145

creates a container for energy to flow into and attract the energy that will fulfill that intention.

This also creates strong energy boundaries, so we don't get distracted by fears or doubts. When you have strong intentions and are focused on your outcomes, you know exactly what you want and ground all of your energy in that outcome. Imagine if you decided to take a road trip to Florida. You do your research, book the hotels, plan the route, and then get in the car. The last thing you do before heading out is to program your destination into your GPS system.

If you're going to Florida, would you program your GPS for Los Angeles?

Of course not, but that's what we do when we don't have strong intentions or big outcomes, and we allow ourselves to get energetically uncongruent by distractions such as fear. And that makes us an easy target for energy and mind control technologies. Their access point into our energy field is through fear and distractions – do you wonder why the news has gotten so negative, there is so much focus on terrorism now, so much effort is made to keep us in a constant state of agitation, and 'crisis actor' has become a new career path for government produced false flag shootings and attacks around the world? Scared people are much more easily manipulated than those who are firmly and fearlessly grounded in their own energy.

When we are energetically congruent we are whole and complete, with all of our energy flowing in the same direction. We are at peace, we align with our joy, we live life on purpose and with intention, and in a way that serves us and our vision of the life we want to have.

We make powerful choices that keep us aligned with our intentions and know that we have a choice in everything. Our lives are balanced and we feel safe and secure because know that we are in control of our energy and through that awareness of how our life is in our control, we cannot be manipulated.

Energetic congruence™ is the new paradigm for our being, it is the new way that we must live our lives if we are going to succeed in the battle for control of our energy. Nothing else is going to override the constant, oppressive presence of energy control technology because we cannot fight against it, we must rise above it. And we must do it individually and collectively.

We no longer have the luxury of being at war with each other, of thinking we are separate and are each others' enemy. The family of humanity shares a common adversary and that is those who are trying to control our energy – nothing is more important today than uniting against this adversary and making a unanimous choice for the peace, joy, love, and prosperity that is the divine right of every human being. Anything else feeds the human energy control protocols machine.

So what happened to the tens and even hundreds of thousands of children that the CIA tested and experimented on during its heyday years? They are in their fifties and sixties today, many of them are beginning to wonder about their lost memories, especially since so much information about mind control testing is being revealed. They have yet to recover, though, and they're often lost, afraid, anxious, and feel out of place, like they don't belong here. Their lives have been difficult, usually lonely, rather unsuccessful as they struggle financially and emotionally – it's hard to create success when you have been implanted with artificial belief that your success comes at the cost of someone else's life, another one of the CIA's psychological torture methods.

That was one of the aspects of the human energy control protocols used on psychically sensitive and high energy children, to separate them from their energy, so they exist on an island of fear surrounded by a sea of doubt. In Anne Diamond's book she mentions some of the testing scenarios that she remembered, where children were forced to hurt animals and each other, children were killed in front of the group, and they were emotionally tortured, shamed, humiliated, and singled out for specific punishments, especially if they protested or refused to participate in the tests, as well as being heavily drugged to erase their memories.

The use of psychological torture to create trauma around speaking up for what is morally right, being socially accepted, and protecting others, was one way that these harbingers of social change were prevented from fully embracing their missions of bringing new light, truth, and transformation to the world. Until now, that is. Because while many of struggled, as I did for years, with trying to break free from the fears that limited their movement, actions, and their voice, as the collective energy expands, these limitations are falling away.

Now that they are beginning to remember, and they are also beginning to get their power back and to reconnect with that inner knowing which reminds them of who they are, no matter what was done to them in the past to prevent that from ever happening. They are becoming congruent with themselves and their mission, and they are deciding to make their own choices about how their energy is used, by others and by themselves.

We must all be willing to embrace our power of 'energetic consent™', which is how we decide to use our energy. This is both an individual and a collective choice. If we, on an individual level, declare that we will use our power of Energetic Consent to have a wonderful, drama free life, we set a boundary that keeps chaos, drama, and trauma out of our life. We also do that for the rest of humanity because what we do for ourselves we also enable for everyone else.

If we, as the family of humanity, declare that we will use our power of Energetic Consent to agree that we will no longer be at war with each other, who is going to fight?

If we, as the family of humanity, declare that we will use our power of Energetic Consent to ensure abundance and prosperity for everyone, who is going to want to be the best, the richest, the most powerful, or have the greatest advantage? And does it really matter anyway? How much does one person need to live on and if that abundance comes at the cost of another's life, security, joy, peace, or livelihood, the price is too high.

You can find a sample Declaration of Energetic Consent™ at the website for this book, humanenergycontrolbook.com.

We have a divine directive to move from uniformity, trying to be the same (which is also a focus of human energy control technology which tries to keep us at the same energy levels that can be manipulated and controlled), to moving into unanimity, which is seeing ourselves as one soul.

We are moving from same-ness, where we try to find similarities in others to find the connection points, to agreeing on our soul-ness, that we are a single soul, expressed as individual humans. When we are unanimous (one soul) we don't need to look for connection points, they are there by default. Then we can be individuals and express our uniqueness because the principle of unanimity negates separation. We all come from the same Source, we all shine under the same Sun, and we are all one in spirit.

We have work to do now, but it's all internal and it's all energetic. It's not 'hard' work, but we do have to put some effort towards it as we work on being energetically congruent – ensuring that our energy is all flowing in the same direction and towards the same outcomes, seeing ourselves as part of the family of humanity and focusing on unanimity, connection, and our 'soul-ness' instead of our differences, and we share a common adversary whose purpose is to keep us in fear, separated, disconnected, and uniform. That makes us more manageable.

What kind of world do you want to live in right now, today, and that you want your children and grandchildren to be able to enjoy? That is the world you can focus on creating for yourself in this moment because now is the time to begin and each step we take towards energetic congruence is another step we take towards having a world whose predominant energies are peace, joy, love, and prosperity for all.

The fate of humanity is not in our hands, so to speak, it is in our energy and we need to begin to reverse the damage that human energy and mind control technology has created and regain control of our energy, our lives, and our planet.

THE FATE OF HUMANITY LIES
WITHIN OUR ENERGY

There is another reason for us to be aware of this technology and take steps to de-activate and remove it, and that involves the fate of humanity. The world is not going to get blown up or end in some catastrophic way. If the non-human, alien, or other manipulative and controlling forces didn't need us, they would have done away with us long ago.

Humanity is still here because we serve a purpose for them, and as devious as that sounds, it is true. They need us and our energy far more than we need them, so we have all of the power in this situation. When we realize that we become invincible and move out of their control sphere.

People who refuse to be manipulated, who know the truth, and who are in control of their energy cannot be manipulated by any means because the strength of the human divinity is far greater than any force of humanity. Now you know the truth, we all know the truth, and we have to decide that we are going to do something about it together.

We can no longer afford the luxury of fear, hate, anger, powerlessness, or discord. Every time we engage in negative emotional energies we feed the fear machine and we give human energy control technologies the advantage over us.

When we decide to focus on our connection, joy, and power we give ourselves the advantage over the technology that needs us to be disconnected, afraid, weak, powerless, unhappy, insecure, and traumatized to be effective.

If we want to live in a world that is ruled by fear and people who believe that they have the right to manipulate human minds and energies for their own purposes, we can continue down the path of fear, hate, anger, and discord and make it easy for them to destroy us using our own energy. And they know this – the only way they can destroy us is to get us to destroy ourselves and each other.

But if we want to live in a world where we co-exist in joy, prosperity, peace, and love, we have to commit to uniting as a global energetic community to make that possible for everyone. We will either be destroyed by our fear or saved by our belief in our own power and sovereignty, and this is a critical moment for us.

If our minds and energy were not so important, creative, and powerful, there would be no reason for these human mind and energy controlling programs to exist. But there is something about the human spirit that is so powerful, so compelling, so special, and so creative, that these people will do anything to gain control over it.

I think that we must be pretty special to deserve so much attention and effort, unwanted though it may be. And we have the means to stop it, so let's do it.

What kind of world do you want to live in? Make that choice now and start creating that in your own life.

Each positive thought you have expands exponentially in all directions, allowing the world to benefit from your positive intention.

And each negative thought you have also expands exponentially in all directions, allowing the world to experience your negativity.

You may think of yourself as small and insignificant, an irrelevant speck in the vast and complex web of humanity's energy field but you are just as significant as every other person on the planet.

The responsibility for humanity's fate lies with each one of us -- we are each significant and important as we make a choice to be in control or to be controlled, to exist in peace, love, joy, and prosperity as the collective family of humanity, or to exist in a controlled darkness of fear, poverty, lack, and chaos.

I urge you to consider this very carefully because human energy control technology is very real, it is being used on us every day, and research into this area is heavily funded by the military and by governments all over the world. But it has its weaknesses and the biggest one is that it cannot work with or on high frequency energy.

That is our only defense against it.

We cannot convince people who are incapable of embodying the qualities of kindness and compassion that they should act with kindness and compassion. Instead, we have to put ourselves beyond their reach and we do that by 'raising our vibes', raising our energy frequency and vibration to levels they and their technology cannot access.

And as a final note, think of the world legacy we will create for our children, grandchildren, and future generations.

How do you want them to live and what kind of world do you want them to inherit from us?

I want my children and their children to enjoy freedom, peace, to be able to know joy, to think independently, and to live long and happy lives. I don't want them to live in an Orwellian society where they are watched, monitored, controlled, and manipulated, although I know that is the truth of our world today, thanks to insightful revelations by whistleblowers such as Julian Assange and Edward Snowden and countless courageous souls who decided that revealing the truth was worth whatever personal price they had to pay, and many have paid with their lives.

I have included a few resources in the final chapter which highlights some of the aspects of energy control technology. Note that these are only the declassified documents so they represent a very small view of this kind of technology and what it is capable of. Also consider that this information points to very devious, manipulative, and perverse actions on the part of our governments and their agencies and if this is what is publicly shared, the truth of what is actually being funded, researched, developed, and used is far more comprehensive and diabolical.

If the CIA thought its mind control experiments were so bad and would create so much opposition that they allegedly destroyed many of the files in the 1970s as information about them began to leak out (although I don't believe they did), imagine what they have hidden in various file cabinets, secret underground military bases, and hidden storage facilities around the world, that they are hiding under the convenient umbrella of 'national security' or 'anti-terrorism' so that no one finds out about what they have been doing in the name of energetic tyranny and global control.

This is our battle to win if we find out the truth and then use it to block all attempts at controlling our energy so we rule our own lives and our world and we can live in unanimous agreement that we want to live in a world whose predominant energies are love, peace, joy, and prosperity for all.

This isn't a topic I normally address and it's a topic that is quite personal for me but I believe that sharing knowledge, information, and experience is one of the most powerful gifts I can give to you. So I am opening a discussion that I hope may help you fill in some of the gaps in your life, as this understanding has helped me with mine.

About Jennifer Hoffman

Jennifer Hoffman is recognized as the world's foremost Energy Savante™ and most accurate intuitive mystic, the leading voice in the ascending spiritual awareness movement for High Vibes Living™, and is an expert in the field of energy resonance, alignment, manifestation, and intention. Paralyzed with GBS at the age of five years, sheer determination allowed her to move and walk again, and she shares her experiences in overcoming life's tragedies to encourage and empower others to rise from their paralyzing and limiting fears and beliefs to create rich, happy, successful lives. She is a business expert with a twenty plus year career in finance, banking, law, technology, technical writing, and software research, , development, testing, and implementation, working in a variety of industries and in companies that ranged from startups to multinational corporations.

She is also a top-selling author, popular radio host, life and business transformation catalyst and spiritual teacher. Since 2004 she has published the weekly Enlightening Life newsletter, with more than 4 million global readers, the Internet's most widely read and shared publication. Jennifer provides life intuition, spiritual wisdom, and business savvy to a client base that includes celebrities, business and industry leaders, professionals and other clients from more than 75 countries.

Jennifer is a life long Intuitive Savante whose unique gifts allow her to read energetic fields and instantly know a client's energy levels, soul purpose, karmic path and life lessons, and what is required to bring their energetic vibrations into alignment with their soul's desire for Energetic Congruence™ in body, mind and spirit. She is recognized for providing highly accurate and focused energetic and intuitive guidance to raise energetic vibrations and create a clear path to joyful, joy-filled, rich, happy and successful living.

Jennifer's work has helped millions connect to and understand their spiritual gifts, find peace on their life journey, and fearlessly connect to their power, to rise above their paralyzing fears and confidently create empowered realities. With over 100,000 customers, Jennifer is the world's most prolific intuitive guide and she continues to provide coaching services to her loyal clientele. Visit enlighteninglife.com to sign up for the celebrated Enlightening Life newsletter and learn more about Jennifer's work, her Energetic Congruence™ programs, and her GPS Business Academy™ business training resources, which are the only business programs taught by an experienced expert in business processes, management, marketing, and business systems.

Resources

I have included some of the human energy control technology resources that I reviewed just to see what was being published on the subject. You can conduct your own search on the internet, just know that much of this information is not published under the topic of 'energy control' but it is included in some of the mind control program information, such as that on MKUltra, Project Monarch, and Beta Programming.

Information about energy control technologies can be found by searching for psychotronic technology and neurotronic weapons and technology. You can also search by technology types, there is a lot of information available on the SSSS, Silent Sound Spread Spectrum, one of the more insidious forms of energy control.

The articles I found date from as early as the 1980s, indicating how long this technology has been in development. It is based on work done by Nicolai Tesla, who patented some of these concepts and this technology in the late 1800s and early 1900s. Much of it was patented and developed during the 1930s and 1940s, with significant done in the 1950s and 1960s, the heyday of energy control technology.

With the exponential nature of technological growth and advancement, and the secretive nature of biomedical, psychotropic and neurotronic technology, you can be assured that what is available now is far more advanced, deliberate, and destructive than the work that was begun with the Nazis and has been conducted in secret for the last seventy years.

===

This is a press release published by Applied Digital Solutions on December 17, 1999 referring to a 'Satellite Tracked Human Implant System' that they have developed.

The device is now called the VeriChip and it is marketed and sold as an implant that stores a patient's medical information for quick access by doctors. It was first voluntarily implanted in humans in 2004.

PALM BEACH, FLORIDA - Applied Digital Solutions, Inc. today announced that it has acquired the patent rights to a miniature digital transceiver - which it has named "Digital Angel" -- that can be used for a variety of purposes, such as providing a tamper-proof means of identification for enhanced e-business security, locating lost or missing individuals, tracking the location of valuable property and monitoring the medical conditions of at-risk patients.

In the agreement signed last week, ADS acquired the right to develop this unique product itself for all of its applications or to sublicense the development of specific applications to other entities. A special technology group has been formed within ADS to supervise the development of the device.

The implantable transceiver sends and receives data and can be continuously tracked by GPS (Global Positioning Satellite) technology. The transceiver's power supply and actuation system are unlike anything ever created. When implanted within a body, the device is powered electromechanically through the movement of muscles, and it can be activated either by the "wearer" or by the monitoring facility. A novel sensation feedback feature will even allow the wearer to control the device to some degree. The "smart" device is also small enough to be hidden inconspicuously on or within valuable personal belongings and priceless works of art.

Commenting on Digital Angel's many potential applications, Richard J. Sullivan, Chairman and CEO of Applied Digital Solutions, Inc. (ADS), said: "We believe its potential for improving individual and e-business security and enhancing the quality of life for millions of people is virtually limitless. Although we're in the early developmental phase, we expect to come forward with applications in many different areas, from medical monitoring to law enforcement. However, in keeping with our core strengths in the e-business to business arena, we plan to focus our initial development efforts on the growing field of e-commerce security and user ID verification."

Sullivan added that the multi-purpose technology would enable ADS to tap into a vast global market, through licensing and other commercial arrangements, with an estimated total value in excess of $100 billion. "The e-business to business security market alone could reach as high as $10 to $12 billion in the near future," Sullivan added.

ADS is actively seeking joint venture partners to help develop and market the unique technology. The company expects to create a working prototype by the end of next year.

Applied Digital Solutions, Inc. is an e-business to business solutions provider offering Internet, telecom, LAN and software services to a wide variety of businesses throughout North America.

For more information, visit the Company's web site at applied-ds.com

===

US Patent 6239705 B1 Intra Oral Tracking Device

This patent covers an implant that is inserted in the mouth and one of its claims is to track 'lost dentures' via GPS satellite positioning. How likely is it that someone would lose their dentures and why would they need a satellite to track them?

The link is here http://www.google.com/patents/US6239705 Scroll down to the bottom of the page and note the Citations and the Reference sections, which mention patents that have similar technical applications.

This is the patent abstract, note the reference to this as a 'stealthy ... tracking device', meaning that the person implanted with the device can be tracked without their knowledge, awareness, or approval:

"An improved stealthy, non-surgical, biocompatible electronic tracking device is provided in which a housing is placed intraorally. The housing contains micro-circuitry. The microcircuitry comprises a receiver, a passive mode to active mode activator, a signal decoder for determining positional fix, a transmitter, an antenna, and a power supply.

Optionally, an amplifier may be utilized to boost signal strength. The power supply energizes the receiver. Upon receiving a coded activating signal, the positional fix signal decoder is energized, determining a positional fix. The transmitter subsequently transmits through the antenna a position locating signal to be received by a remote locator.

In another embodiment of the present invention, the microcircuitry comprises a receiver, a passive mode to active mode activator, a transmitter, an antenna and a power supply. Optionally, an amplifier may be utilized to boost signal strength. The power supply energizes the receiver. Upon receiving a coded activating signal, the transmitter is energized. The transmitter subsequently transmits through the antenna a homing signal to be received by a remote locator."

===

For more information on mind and energy control technology, its applications, and some research, visit

http://www.constitution.org/abus/mkt/uncom.htm#IMPLA

This website provides an overview of this technology but it is not current and many of the links refer to outdated or unavailable pages. It does, however, show how extensive this technology is, where it is used, and its applications that were being considered nearly twenty years ago.

===

Devices can be implanted in the human body that require no wires or batteries because they are charged by the same natural electronic transmissions that allow muscle movement. And they are proudly announced by scientists and researchers, irrespective of the dangers of these technologies and their dubious and sinister potential applications. While the applications they mention are medical and designed to alleviate the suffering caused by disease, their other applications, such as use for energy, mind, and brain control, are not mentioned.

Here's a BBC news article from October 15, 1998, describing 'bionic brain implants' that work with human thought. Note how the implant is able to access the body's neural fibers (nerves) so it becomes a permanent fixture within the body. These implants are capable of both receiving and transmitting signals, providing access to the body's functioning at all levels.

If the implant can be controlled by thought, the implant can also be used to control thought.

Here is a link to the article which was available as of this printing.

http://news.bbc.co.uk/2/hi/sci/tech/193946.stm

=====================================

Bionic brain implants allowing a computer to be operated by the power of thought have been developed by American scientists. Researchers at Emory University in Atlanta, Georgia, achieved the breakthrough by implanting hollow glass cone electrodes inside the brain's motor cortex - the part of the brain which controls movement - into which nerve cells grow and attach themselves.

Two severely disabled volunteers who received the implants were able to control the cursor on a computer screen just by thinking about moving parts of their body. Pointing the cursor at particular icons allowed them to communicate, making the computer voice phrases such as "I'm thirsty" or "please turn off the light".

The team hopes that as the technique is developed, the icons on the computer screen could perform more advanced functions, such as moving an artificial limb. Simply by thinking of the movement, the computer could do what the body no longer can.

However, the leader of the team, Dr Philip Kennedy, said the system would not be widely available for some time. "It is going to take many more patients ... I don't think people should get their hopes up too high yet. I think it's going to take several years," he said.

Each implant consists of a hollow glass cone about the size of a ball-point pen tip. The cones are laced with neurotrophic chemicals extracted from the patient's own knees which encourage nerve growth. Over several months, the implant becomes naturally 'wired' into the patient's brain as neurones grow into the cones and attach themselves to the electrodes mounted inside.

When the person thinks of an action which would normally occur through the nervous system, it is transmitted from the electrode to the computer. An FM transmitter under the scalp transmits the signal without wires, and power induction means no batteries are needed.

"We transmit that out, process the signals, feed it back to the patient, so he can hear the activity, and also see the cursor move. So he is learning to move the cursor from one icon to the other," Dr Kennedy explained.

The first volunteer was a woman with Lou Gehrig's disease, a neurodegenerative condition that gradually robs victims of their ability to move. She received the implants 18 months ago and has since died of her disease. A second volunteer, a 57-year-old man almost totally paralysed by a stroke, received the implants six months ago.

The team has now been promised funding by the US National Institutes of Health to continue the research with three more patients.

=====================================

And check out these patents and their descriptions:

U.S. Patent 5,159,703 – SILENT SUBLIMINAL PRESENTATION SYSTEM

U.S. Patent 5,507,291 – METHOD AND AN ASSOCIATED APPARATUS FOR REMOTELY DETERMINING INFORMATION AS TO A PERSON'S EMOTIONAL STATE.

U.S. Patent US5629678: IMPLANTABLE TRANSECEIVER – Apparatus for Tracking and Recovering Humans.

U.S. Patent 6,014,080 – BODY WORN ACTIVE AND PASSIVE TRACKING DEVICE.

U.S. Patent 5,868,100 – FENCELESS ANIMAL CONTROL SYSTEM USING GPS (Global Positioning Satellite) LOCATION INFORMATION.

And here is another US patent, this one is for an 'Apparatus and Method for Remotely Monitoring and Altering Brain Waves'. It's US Patent 3,951,134 filed on April 20, 1976.

Here is the abstract and note the last sentence, which describes how the implant can also receive signals and alter brain activity:

US PATENT 3,951,134 - APPARATUS AND METHOD FOR REMOTELY MONITORING AND ALTERING BRAIN WAVES

Apparatus for and method of sensing brain waves at a position remote from a subject whereby electromagnetic signals of different frequencies are simultaneously transmitted to the brain of the subject in which the signals interfere with one another to yield a waveform which is modulated by the subject's brain waves. The interference waveform which is representative of the brain wave activity is re-transmitted by the brain to a receiver where it is demodulated and amplified. The demodulated waveform is then displayed for visual viewing and routed to a computer for further processing and analysis. The demodulated waveform also can be used to produce a compensating signal which is transmitted back to the brain to effect a desired change in electrical activity therein.

==

This is a lengthy description of the history of psychotronic weapons systems, which use microwaves, sound, energy frequency generators, and described in 2001 by Representative Dennis Kucinich as "enabling access to human brain, human health impairment or killing of people ... land-based, sea-based or space-based systems using radiation, electromagnetic, psychotronic, sonic, laser or other energies directed at individual persons or targeted populations for the purpose of information war, mood managment or mind control of such persons or population."

This document, titled "Means of Information War Threaten Democracy and Mankind" by Mojimir Babacek, has been published and removed from the internet a number of times because it is a compilation of the history of mind and energy control methods, systems, uses, and plans by the U.S. and other countries for four decades.

http://www.opednews.com/articles/Means-of-Information-War-T-by-mojmir-Babacek-090713-819.html

LA Times article, January 2015, on Veteran suicide rate statistics:

http://www.latimes.com/nation/la-na-veteran-suicide-20150115-story.html

A timeline of mind control experimentation, beginning in the 1930s to 1999

http://www.bibliotecapleyades.net/esp_cointelpro06.htm

A list of the top secret government projects with a brief overview of what they do

http://in5d.com/top-secret-government-programs-that-your-not-supposed-to-know-about/

Here is a Wiki List of some of the world's most famous whistle-blowers, people who were willing to step forward and expose corruption, abuse, and wrong doing in the world.

https://en.wikipedia.org/wiki/List_of_whistleblowers

~~~~~~

Here is a site which describes the link between HDTV and SSSS (Silent Sound Spread Spectrum) technology:

http://wariscrime.com/new/digital-tv-mind-control-by-the-sound-of-silence/

And here is Patent #5159703, note the abstract, which has been quoted I this article, as well as the referring patents at the bottom of the page

http://www.google.com/patents/US5159703

Note the applicants for those patents, some are held by individuals, others are held by companies such as IBM,

The referring patents are the components that this technology uses which have already been patented by other people.

Note the language in the German patent number DE 102012009060 A1, which other mind and energy control patents refer to.

"Method for influencing subconscious mind through audio suggestion   for changing acquired behavior of user, involves inputting information tailored to changing behavior in acoustic device, and converting information into acoustic information"

And look at the companies holding referral patents, a who's who of global multinationals, IBM, Sony, Microsoft, Martin Marietta, and NEC.

20392407R00107

Printed in Great Britain
by Amazon